THE
KINGFISHER
CHILDREN'S
ENCYCLOPEDIA

3

Constellation – Explorer

KING*f*ISHER

KINGFISHER
Kingfisher Publications Plc
New Penderel House
283-288 High Holborn
London WC1V 7HZ
www.kingfisherpub.co.uk

First published by Kingfisher Publications Plc in 1998
This updated edition published in 2004

10 9 8 7 6 5 4 3 2 1

1TS/1104/C&C/(MAR)/128MA/F

A CIP catalogue record for this book is available from
the British Library

ISBN 0-7534-1193-8
Printed in China

The websites listed in this book are correct at the time of publishing. However,
due to the ever-changing nature of the internet, website addresses and content
can change. Websites can contain links that are unsuitable for children. The publisher
cannot be held responsible for changes in website addresses or content, or for
information obtained through third-party websites. We strongly advise that
internet searches should be supervised by an adult.

INTRODUCTION

The word *encyclopedia* comes from the Greek for 'all-round education', and *The Kingfisher Children's Encyclopedia* provides just that, in a way that is both accessible and stimulating.

This all-new encyclopedia covers everything from ancient history to up-to-the-minute developments in technology; from animal and plant life on Earth to plans for the next millennium in outer space. Geography, natural history, religion, the human body – all the topics that children explore at home and at school are included here.

We have rejected the 'sound-bite' approach to children's reference in favour of more in-depth coverage, which makes this encyclopedia perfect for project work and homework assignments. At the same time, the text is broken up into manageable paragraphs, suitable for both confident readers and younger browsers. Colourful photographs and superb illustrations and maps not only enhance the text, but also encourage readers to find out more for themselves.

Easy access is the key to this encyclopedia. Major subject areas such as ELECTRICITY have been arranged alphabetically, but the encyclopedia also has a comprehensive index so that readers can refer quickly to related topics, such as CIRCUITS and SWITCHES.

The encyclopedia has been written and checked by a team of specialist authors and consultants, and produced by a team of editors and designers with years of experience in children's reference. We are confident that it is a book in which children, and parents, can put their trust.

The Editors

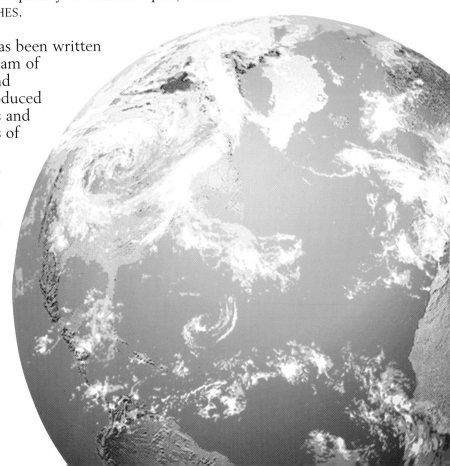

Editorial Director
Jennifer Justice

Managing Editor
Sarah Allen

Editorial team
Trevor Anderson, Max Benato, Jane Birch,
Harry Boteler, Anne Davies, Rebecca Fry, Aimee Johnson,
Tracey Kelly, Sarah Kovandzich, Elizabeth Longley,
Miren Lopategui, Rupert Matthews, Jayne Miller, Brian Williams

Creative Director
Val Pidgeon

Art Director
Mike Davis

Art Editor
David Noon

Design team
Liz Black, Pete Byrne, John Jamieson,
Ruth Levy, Emma Skidmore, Nina Tara

Picture Research
Veneta Bullen, Davina Bullen,
Sophie Mortimer, Yannick Yago

Maps
Hardlines

Contributors & Consultants
Sue Aldridge, Sarah Angliss, Max Benato,
Martyn Bramwell, Enid Broderick, Tim Brown,
David Burnie, Catherine Halcrow, Jack Challoner, Michael Chinery,
Maria Constantino, Chris Cooper, Sophie Cooper, Alan Cowsill,
Jeff Daniel, David Darling, Dougal Dixon, John Farndon,
Sue Gordon, John Graham, Ian Graham, Catherine Headlam,
Lesley Hill, Caroline Juler, Anne Kay, Robin Kerrod,
J.C. Levy, Keith Lye, Tim Madge, David Marshall, Bob McCabe,
Iain Nicolson, Steve Parker, Jane Parker, John Paton,
Malcolm Porter, Sue Reid, Meg Sanders, Bill Shapiro,
Philip Steele, Richard Tames, John Tipler,
Ian Westwell, Brian Williams

CONSTELLATION

Constellations are groups of stars that form recognizable patterns in the night sky. Astronomers have named a total of 88 constellations.

▲ The Northern and Southern Hemispheres are domes of sky seen above and below the Equator.

Thousands of years ago, people in Asia, Europe and the Middle East realized that the stars formed patterns in the sky, and named them after characters and creatures in their lives and legends. By AD300, the Greek astronomer Ptolemy had named 48 constellations. Many of the names he gave them are still in use, including Taurus (the Bull), Ursa Major (the Great Bear) and Andromeda (a mythical Ancient Greek heroine). Today, astronomers use the position of the constellations to map the stars.

THE ZODIAC

If we could see the stars during the day, the Sun would pass in front of 13 constellations over the course of the year. The ancient astronomers counted only 12 constellations and called them the signs of the zodiac – claiming that babies born under each sign would have certain traits.

NEAR AND FAR

Stars in a constellation seem close to each other, but are usually far apart. Orion contains the stars Betelgeuse (300 light years away from Earth), Rigel (900 light years away) and Mintaka (2,300 light years away). One light year equals 9.46 million million kilometres.

MAPS OF THE STARS

Two maps of the constellations are needed because people who live north of the Equator (in the Northern Hemisphere) see different stars from those who live south of the Equator (in the Southern Hemisphere). The constellations in the centre of both maps can usually be seen all year round, while those near the edge can be seen only during particular seasons or at certain times of the night.

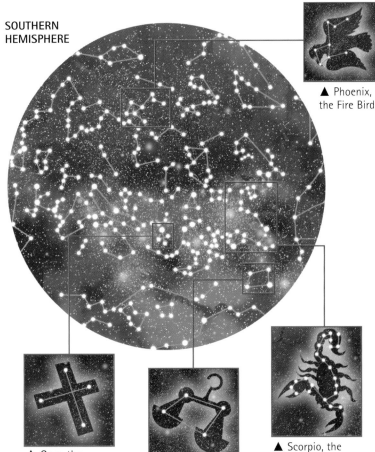

SOUTHERN HEMISPHERE

NORTHERN HEMISPHERE

▲ Pegasus, the Flying Horse

▲ Phoenix, the Fire Bird

▲ Crux, the Southern Cross

▲ Libra, the Scales

▲ Scorpio, the Scorpion

▲ Hercules, the Giant

▲ Ursa Major, the Great Bear

▲ Leo, the Lion

SEE ALSO

Astronomy, Galaxy, Myth and legend, Solar system, Star

CONSTRUCTION

Construction is the process of putting something together. It includes erecting houses, skyscrapers, bridges, dams and roads, as well as building ships.

▲ Hong Kong Harbour Bridge under construction in 1996. The last road section is being lifted from a barge below.

Bricks are still the most popular construction material in house building.

The construction industry is big business – it accounts for 15 per cent of all jobs in the United States. The world's largest construction project, building a city in Saudi Arabia in the late 1970s, employed nearly 52,000 people.

TRADITIONAL TECHNIQUES
In the past, most construction was domestic – each family built a house, pens for animals and dams to irrigate their crops. The materials were usually natural and found locally, and included wood, clay, stone, bone, skin or grass. Work was done by hand.

Carpentry is used to make the main frame, doors and windows in many houses.

THE DAWN OF CIVILIZATION
As more complex civilizations developed, so did building skills. The first bricks were made in Palestine in 6000BC, and the construction of the pyramids in Egypt required thousands of workers, as well as skilled mathematicians. Ancient cranes were used on Roman building sites.

The frames of tall buildings and ships used to be fixed with hot nails, or rivets.

MODERN CONSTRUCTION
The size and height of constructions used to be limited by the skill of the stonemason or carpenter. But from the late 1800s, new techniques using steel frames and moulded concrete allowed skyscrapers to be built.

A BUILDING GOES UP
There are two main stages in constructing a building. First, the foundations must be laid below ground to support the structure. Tough materials are used, such as concrete (poured in trenches) or steel columns (driven into the ground). The second stage is the construction of the building above ground. Either the walls or a steel frame are constructed first to support floors and other features. Finally, the roof is added.

STEEL-FRAMED CONSTRUCTION
Modern high-rise buildings usually have a steel frame onto which floors and wall panels are bolted. The frame supports the weight of the building so walls can be thin with large windows.

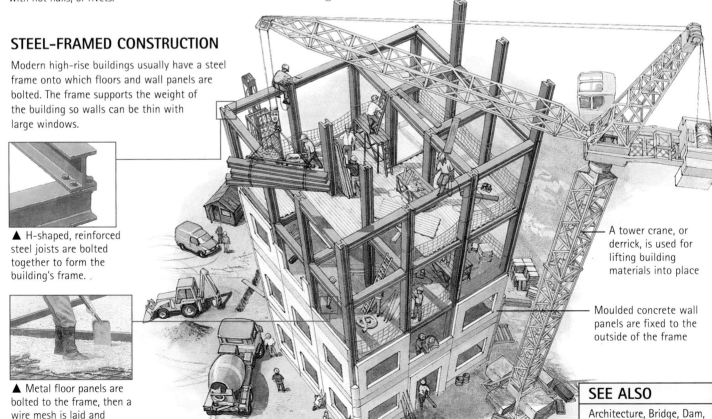

▲ H-shaped, reinforced steel joists are bolted together to form the building's frame.

▲ Metal floor panels are bolted to the frame, then a wire mesh is laid and concrete is poured over it.

A tower crane, or derrick, is used for lifting building materials into place

Moulded concrete wall panels are fixed to the outside of the frame

SEE ALSO
Architecture, Bridge, Dam, Egypt (Ancient), Road, Ship, Skyscraper, Tunnel

CONTINENT

Continents are large stretches of land unbroken by sea. There are seven continents on Earth.

The continents are attached to tectonic plates, the pieces which form the Earth's surface.

HOW CONTINENTS DRIFT

All the land on Earth is fixed to giant plates which float on a sea of magma (melted rock). As the magma moves slowly, so do the continents, but some towards each other and others apart. Where two giant plates rub together, a crack sometimes appears in the Earth's surface, allowing magma to escape. Two such cracks, known as mid-ocean ridges, run through the Atlantic and Indian oceans.

As it moves, the plate cracks to form fault lines

The Earth's crust is like a giant jigsaw puzzle made up of eight large pieces and several small pieces, called tectonic plates. On top of these plates sit seven land masses, or continents: Africa, Antarctica, Asia, Australia, Europe, North America and South America. Together they make up 95 per cent of Earth's land surface, with islands forming the rest. The largest continent is Asia, with an area of just over 44 million sq km, and the smallest is Australia, covering about 7.7 million sq km.

CONTINENTAL CRUST

The continents are the thickest parts of the Earth's outer layer, or crust – in some places reaching down 60km to 70km. At the centre, the continents contain the oldest rocks on the planet, with some dating back three billion years. As newer rocks were added around the fringes of these ancient cores, the continents grew.

FLOATING WORLD

The tectonic plates on which the continents sit are floating on a hot, molten layer called magma. Heat from deep inside the Earth keeps the magma moving slowly, and as it moves, so do the plates and continents. The slow movement of the continents is called continental drift.

VANISHED LANDS

More than 300 million years ago, all the land on Earth formed just one continent, called Pangaea. Then, about 180 million years ago, it split into two continents, called Gondwanaland and Laurasia. Slowly, North and South America broke away, India joined Asia, and Australia split from Antarctica and moved northwards, until today's seven continents were created.

TOMORROW'S CONTINENTS

The movement is still continuing, and the continents we know today will look very different in 50 million years' time. Africa and the Americas, for example, will be even farther away from each other. North and South America will no longer be joined and Australia will have moved farther northwards.

▼ At first there was just one large continent, then two, and finally today's seven continents were formed.

180 million years ago

65 million years ago

SEE ALSO

Africa, Antarctica, Asia, Australia, Earth, Europe, North America, Ocean and sea, Rock, South America

99

CRAB AND OTHER CRUSTACEANS

Crabs belong to a group of animals called crustaceans. These creatures have no bones and are covered with a hard shell called an exoskeleton.

The male fiddler crab has a very large claw, which it waves as part of a display to attract the female.

The hermit crab lives in an empty seashell, which it drags around with its two pairs of walking legs.

The lobster has one narrow claw for slicing dead fish, and a heavier claw for crushing clams.

The crayfish grows up to 40cm long, lives in fresh water and has ten legs, like lobsters and crabs.

The water flea is one of the smallest crustaceans, growing to between 0.2mm and 18mm long.

The woodlouse is the only crustacean that lives entirely on land. It can roll itself up for defence.

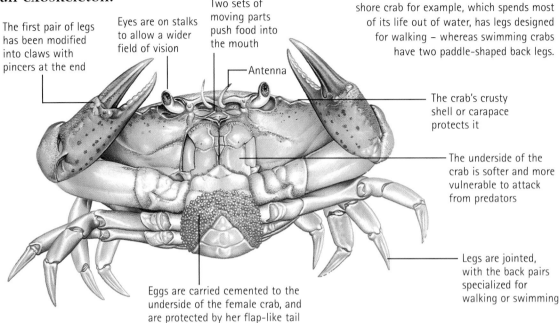

The first pair of legs has been modified into claws with pincers at the end

Eyes are on stalks to allow a wider field of vision

Two sets of moving parts push food into the mouth

Antenna

The crab's crusty shell or carapace protects it

The underside of the crab is softer and more vulnerable to attack from predators

Legs are jointed, with the back pairs specialized for walking or swimming

Eggs are carried cemented to the underside of the female crab, and are protected by her flap-like tail

LIVING ON THE SHORELINE

Most crabs live in or near the sea, but many have adapted to life on land. The shore crab for example, which spends most of its life out of water, has legs designed for walking – whereas swimming crabs have two paddle-shaped back legs.

Crustaceans include shrimps, lobsters, woodlice, water fleas and barnacles. Altogether, there are about 42,000 species of crustacean. Beneath its hard body shell, a crustacean's body is divided into sections, with jointed legs attached. Crabs, lobsters and barnacles have especially thick shells, which contain a lot of chalk-like material. This makes their shells feel like crusts.

EYES ON STALKS

There are about 4,500 species of crab. The smallest are the tiny pea crabs, which are less than 1cm across. The biggest are spider crabs, which live on the sea bed and measure up to 4m across from the tip of one leg to another. Crabs have ten legs, two of which are claws, and their eyes can move up and down on the end of stalks.

CRAB HABITS

Crabs usually live in water or close to the shore. Large crabs feed mainly on dead animals, which they tear up with their claws, while small crabs pick tiny scraps of food from the sea bed. Many crabs move sideways on land. The robber crab climbs palm trees to pick young coconuts, which it bores into with its powerful claws.

WITHOUT A SHELL

A crab's body is armoured by a shell which moults as the crab grows. The hermit crab, however, does not have a shell and must inhabit empty mollusc shells to protect its soft abdomen. As it grows, it searches for a bigger shell to make its home.

HATCHED FROM EGGS

Crabs and other crustaceans reproduce by laying eggs. On hatching, the tiny larvae drift about in water, passing through several body changes before they become adults. In a few species, such as the woodlouse, the young hatch out looking like mini adults.

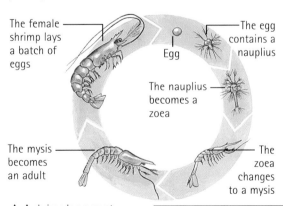

The female shrimp lays a batch of eggs

Egg

The egg contains a nauplius

The nauplius becomes a zoea

The zoea changes to a mysis

The mysis becomes an adult

▲ A shrimp larva must pass through several stages before becoming an adult.

SEE ALSO
Animal, Seashore

CROP

Crops are plants that people grow in fields, to provide food such as wheat and potatoes or other useful materials such as cotton and linen.

◀ Cotton is a cash crop. It is grown for its fibres, which are spun to make fabric or cotton wool. Its seeds are also crushed to produce oil and fodder.

Wheat grows worldwide, in areas with moist mild winters and dry summers.

Rice grows best in warm, wet areas such as China, where it is a staple food.

Potatoes, originally from Peru, have long been an important crop in Europe.

Sugar beet is grown for its sugar-rich root. Its leaves are used as animal fodder.

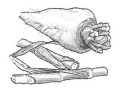

Coffee is the major cash crop in tropical regions. It is grown on plantations.

Grapes are grown in vineyards and harvested for wine, raisins and fresh fruit.

The type of crop grown by farmers depends on the climate of the country, the quality of the soil and its demand in the market. In developing countries, especially in tropical parts of the world, people grow just enough of a crop for their own needs. These are called subsistence crops. Other people, usually farmers, grow large amounts of crops, so that they can be sold. These are called cash crops.

ESSENTIAL CEREALS

The most important food crops are cereals – large grasses grown for their seeds or grains. Cereals include wheat, rice, maize, oats, sorghum and millet, which cover about three quarters of the world's farmland. Wheat is the most popular cereal, with about 590 million tonnes grown every year, mainly for humans to eat, but also as animal feed. Rice is the main ingredient in the diet of over half the world's people, particularly in Asia.

ROOTS TO FRUITS

Another vital food source are the root crops – plants with edible fleshy roots. The potato is an important root crop in Europe, and yams and cassavas are staples in many parts of Africa. Cotton and flax are grown for their fibrous flowers which are used to make cotton and linen. Other major crops include tea and tobacco, which are grown for their leaves, and fruit such as bananas and apples.

WILD ANCESTORS

All crops have come from wild plants, but they have been bred over time to provide bigger and better yields in soils or climates that are not their natural home. Some crops have changed so much that it is hard to say which wild plants were their ancestors. As field and crop sizes have grown, the use of fertilizers, insecticides and fungicides has also risen.

HARVESTING THE CROP

Combine harvesters automatically cut, thresh and clean cereals such as wheat ready for transportation to market. Special attachments can be added to harvest different crops such as soya beans and maize.

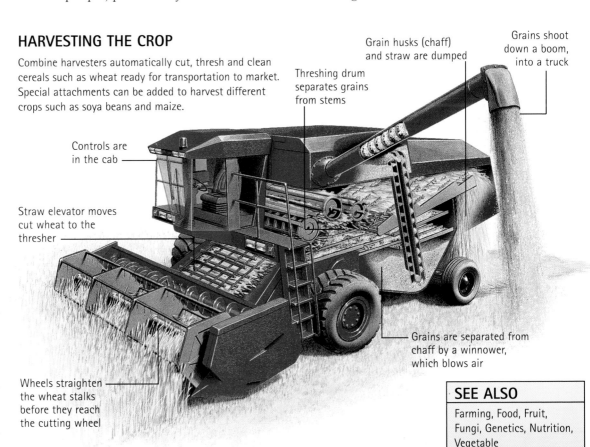

Grain husks (chaff) and straw are dumped

Grains shoot down a boom, into a truck

Threshing drum separates grains from stems

Controls are in the cab

Straw elevator moves cut wheat to the thresher

Grains are separated from chaff by a winnower, which blows air

Wheels straighten the wheat stalks before they reach the cutting wheel

SEE ALSO

Farming, Food, Fruit, Fungi, Genetics, Nutrition, Vegetable

CRUSADES

The Crusades were a series of religious wars that took place in the Holy Land in the Middle Ages. They were fought between Christians and Muslims.

Nuredin was the Muslim leader who united the Islamic forces that Saladin took into battle at Hattin.

For nearly 200 years, starting in 1096, Christians from Europe marched to Palestine to fight the Muslims for control of the Holy Land, especially Jerusalem. They carried the Pope's blessing, but many fought for power and wealth.

THE BEGINNING

From the 7th century, Muslim Arabs ruled the Holy Land, but Christian pilgrims were allowed to visit Jerusalem. Then, in 1071, the Muslim Turks captured Jerusalem and threatened the Christian Byzantine Empire. Pope Urban II called for Christian soldiers to unite and march to the Holy Land to recapture Jerusalem and protect pilgrims.

PILGRIM PEASANTS

The response to the Pope's call was vast. With cries of *Deus Vult!* (meaning 'God wills it' in Latin), thousands of people began the long march eastwards. The first to set out for the Byzantine capital of Constantinople were bands of poorly armed pilgrim peasants under the leadership of Peter the Hermit and Walter the Penniless. Many died on the way, and the

Sultan Saladin led the united Muslim armies and took Christian strongholds after the Second Crusade.

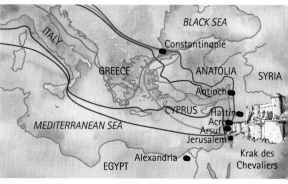

▲ The Crusaders travelled to the Holy Land by land and sea from all the Christian kingdoms of Europe. They built more than 100 castles and fortresses in the area. One of the best preserved is Krak des Chevaliers in Syria, which withstood 12 sieges before falling to the Muslims in 1271.

——— First Crusade (1096–99)
——— Second Crusade (1147–49)
——— Third Crusade (1188–92)
——— Fourth Crusade (1202–4)

rest were killed by the Muslims as soon as they reached Anatolia.

AN ARMY OF KNIGHTS

The First Crusade began in November 1096, when a large army, mostly consisting of French and Norman knights under the leadership of noblemen such as Godfrey de Bouillon, gathered at Constantinople. The army defeated the Muslims, capturing the cities of Antioch and Jerusalem, and establishing a Christian kingdom along the Palestinian and Syrian coast.

THE BATTLE OF ARSUF

In 1191, King Richard I secured victory over the Muslim leader Saladin at Arsuf, with a charge of armoured knights. The charge was led by the Knights Templars and Knights Hospitallers – two military orders of skilled knights who were fanatical enemies of Islam and, like monks, took religious vows.

JERUSALEM IS LOST

Muslim counterattacks started the Second Crusade (1147–49), in which King Louis VII of France and King Conrad II of Germany led separate attacks on Anatolia. These ended in failure for the Christians and weakened their hold on the Holy Land. In 1187, a new Muslim leader, Saladin, led Islamic opposition and wiped out the Crusaders at the Battle of the Horns of Hattin. He then captured Jerusalem and most of the Holy Land.

RICHARD THE LIONHEART

The Third Crusade (1189–92) was led by Richard I (Richard the Lionheart of England), Frederick I of Germany, and Philip II of France. Unfortunately, Frederick drowned on the way, but the Crusaders defeated Saladin and retook much of the Holy Land, except Jerusalem.

LATER CRUSADES

The Fourth Crusade (1202–4) ended in chaos. Its leaders wanted power and riches, and concentrated on Constantinople instead of fighting for the Holy

Land. The Christians had little success in the Fifth Crusade (1217–21), but gained Jerusalem by treaty during the Sixth (1222–29). The Seventh Crusade (1248–54) ended with the capture of Louis IX of France, who was freed only after a ransom was paid.

FINAL BATTLE

During the Eighth Crusade (1270–72), the Muslims continued to advance. In 1291, they secured the last of the vital ports of Acre. No more Crusades took place and many of the knights settled on the island of Cyprus.

In 1212, thousands of children went on a children's crusade to the Holy Land. They did not reach their destination and many of them died or were sold as slaves.

King Richard I of England led the Third Crusade and was given the nickname 'Richard the Lionheart'.

Louis IX ruled the coast around Acre, Syria, for four years between the Seventh and Eighth Crusades.

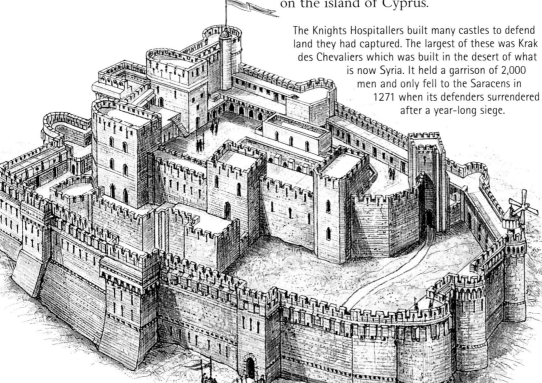

The Knights Hospitallers built many castles to defend land they had captured. The largest of these was Krak des Chevaliers which was built in the desert of what is now Syria. It held a garrison of 2,000 men and only fell to the Saracens in 1271 when its defenders surrendered after a year-long siege.

SEE ALSO

Castle, Christianity, Empire, Islam, Middle Ages, Middle East, Warfare

CUSTOM

Customs are the traditions, rituals and ways of behaving in a society which are passed on from generation to generation and are sometimes turned into laws.

Some Portuguese fishermen paint eyes on their boats to watch over them at sea and bring them back safely.

The *haka*, performed by New Zealand rugby teams before a match, is based on a Maori war dance.

The custom of carving pumpkin faces comes from the Celtic Day of the Dead, celebrated on October 31st.

The *chanoyu*, a Japanese tea ceremony which can last for four hours, came originally from China.

The painting of eggs is a symbol of new life which has been adopted by Christians at Easter time.

DANCING DRAGON

During the Chinese New Year festival, dancers inside a dragon costume move through the streets while fire crackers are set off. The dragon is believed to bring rain for a successful crop and so has become a symbol of good fortune for the coming year. The fire crackers are to frighten away evil spirits.

Every society has its own set of customs, whether it is waiting in a queue, or wearing a particular costume during a celebration. Learning about different customs helps us to understand people from other countries or cultures.

RITES OF PASSAGE

Across the world, customs are different, but there are times of life, known as rites of passage, when a person's status changes. Such times include birth, coming of age, marriage and death – occasions that are marked by elaborate customs in every society. The custom of keeping mother and baby secluded from society for a month after birth is a common custom in many countries, probably based on fear of infection. There are also many customs marking a young person's move from childhood to adulthood, ranging from throwing a party to a religious ritual.

LINKS WITH THE PAST

Customs may be adapted over time, often due to industrialization or contact with other cultures. A custom's original meaning may be forgotten, or it may continue as a way of keeping a link with the past. In the USA, for example, families hold special meals at Thanksgiving to celebrate the first harvest of the Pilgrim Fathers, even though few people today are farmers.

CUSTOMARY GREETINGS

Everyday customs help people to bond with other members of their society. For instance, every culture has a customary way of greeting – Europeans kiss or shake hands, the Inuit rub noses and the Chinese bow. By taking part in customs, people demonstrate their membership of a group or society.

GOING AGAINST THE GRAIN

Refusing to follow a custom can offend, and may lead to the exclusion of an individual from a group of society. Customs are not laws, but because they are designed to help us understand what is acceptable behaviour in a society, they are often included in laws or religious codes.

▲ In Hindu weddings, everything is brightly coloured, and the bride usually wears a red sari with lots of gold jewellery.

SEE ALSO
Clothing, Dance, Judaism

DAM

A dam is a barrier built across a river or stream to hold back water. The stored water may be used for irrigation, as drinking water, or to provide power.

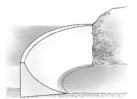

Arch dams, used in tall, narrow canyons or gorges, are often surprisingly thin.

Concrete gravity dams are built to hold back water in broad, shallow valleys.

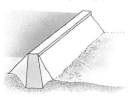

Embankment dams have a reinforced inner wall to hold back shallow lakes.

The earliest dams were built in the Middle East about 5,000 years ago. These dams were used to direct water to fields of crops, through canals called irrigation channels. A dam built on the Orontes River in Syria about 1300BC still irrigates fields near the city of Homs.

CONTROLLING THE FLOW

Today, dams are still built for irrigation, as well as to stop flooding and to provide water power for electricity. In low-lying areas of China, Bangladesh and the USA, dams have been built to stop flood disasters. Other dams are built so that water can be stored in artificial lakes called reservoirs. The water is then supplied to homes and industry.

HYDROELECTRIC DAM

Hydroelectric dams use water power to produce electricity. They require large quantities of water and a very long drop from the top to the bottom of the dam. About 20 per cent of the world's electricity is generated by hydroelectric dams.

EMBANKMENT DAMS

The simplest dams are embankment dams. They are made from earth and rock and have a waterproof core to stop water seeping through. The Aswan High Dam in Egypt controls the annual flooding of the River Nile as well as providing hydroelectric power for the whole country.

GRAVITY AND ARCH

Gravity dams are made of stone or concrete. They rely on their weight and strength to hold back the water. Arch dams are curved so that the weight of the water is pushed out from the dam to the canyon or gorge. This means they can be very thin – for example, the Vaiont Dam in the Italian Alps is 265m high but only 23m thick at its base.

ENVIRONMENTAL IMPACT

Dam-building affects the surrounding environment, and wildlife can be destroyed. Some dams have fish ladders, which enable fish such as salmon to make their journey upstream to breed.

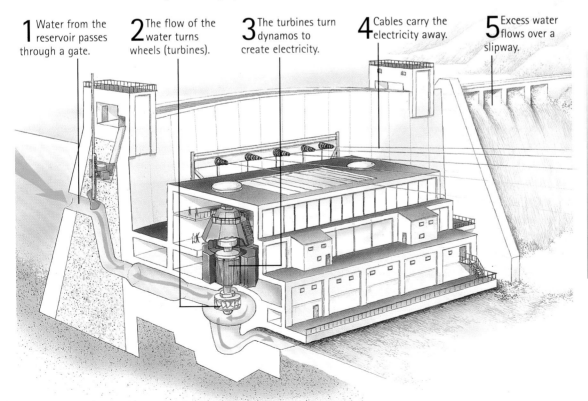

1 Water from the reservoir passes through a gate.

2 The flow of the water turns wheels (turbines).

3 The turbines turn dynamos to create electricity.

4 Cables carry the electricity away.

5 Excess water flows over a slipway.

FAST FACTS

• The world's biggest dam is the Syncrude Tailings Dam in Alberta, Canada

• At 167m high, the Grand Coulee Dam, which blocks the Columbia River, USA, is 20m taller than the Great Pyramid in Egypt

• Dams were so important in ancient Mesopotamia that King Hammurabi's laws said that anyone who broke a dam should be sold into slavery to pay the farmer

SEE ALSO

Construction, Egypt, Water power

DANCE

Dance is one of the oldest art forms. It is the rhythmic movement of all or part of the body, and includes ballet, the waltz, flamenco, tap, rumba and disco.

Dancing can express emotion, tell a story, create a specific atmosphere or show off physical strength. There are two main types of dance: social dancing for enjoyment, and dance created to entertain an audience.

DANCING THROUGH HISTORY

People have been dancing for thousands of years – dancing figures appear in cave paintings in Europe and Africa dating back to prehistoric times. Many of the earliest dances that are still popular today were connected with religious ceremonies or superstitious beliefs. English morris dancing is based on ancient war rituals and voodoo dancers in Haiti go into a trance in which they attempt to summon the spirits. The expressive dance drama of the Ancient Greeks has had a long-lasting influence in the West.

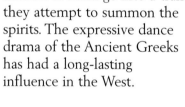

► Ice-skating competitions feature ice dancing in their freestyle section. Couples are not allowed to lift one another, but often imitate traditional ballroom dance routines using daring athletic poses.

GETTING TOGETHER

Formal social dances, where set steps are followed, go back many centuries. Bugaku dancing in Japan originated in the 7th century. In medieval Europe, grand social dances were popular at court. Most were adapted from the simple country dances of ordinary people. As early as the 15th century, there were dance teachers who taught the steps to the latest dances.

CLASSIC BEAUTY

Ballet originated in the royal courts of Italy during the 1400s, but was developed in France. King Louis XIV was an enthusiastic dancer, and opened the first European dance academy in Paris in 1661. Until then, most dancers had been amateur, but professional dancers soon began to appear. The academy's director, Charles-Louis Beauchamp, helped to standardize the classic movements. He is thought to have set out the five basic ballet positions of the feet and arms. By the mid-1800s, romantic ballets such as *La Sylphide* were popular in Europe.

▲ Contemporary dance is less structured than ballet and does not always tell a story. It often uses choreography of the dancers' bodies to form striking poses.

▼ Ballet tells a story, whether it is a classical tale such as *Swan Lake*, or a favourite children's story like *Alice in Wonderland*. Here, Alice (far right) meets the fearsome Queen of Hearts during her journey through Wonderland.

◀ Music and dance are important in the cultures of many tribal countries, such as Zimbabwe, Africa. Here a Shangaan dancer, in an elaborate costume with wings, mask and grass skirt, performs a tribal dance.

▲ Dancing to repetitive music with a powerful underlying beat, often in strobe lighting, swept clubs in the 1990s.

BREAKING AWAY

The second half of the 1800s was the era of classical Russian ballet, with great masterpieces such as Tchaikovsky's *Swan Lake*. But by the early 1900s, some dancers were beginning to create a freer style, breaking away from the rigid patterns and training of classical ballet. The American dancer Isadora Duncan was a big influence on contemporary dance. She performed barefoot, basing her moves on ideas inspired by Ancient Greece.

TAKE YOUR PARTNERS

As time went by, trends in social dances changed along with styles of music. In the 1800s, the waltz caused a scandal because the man and woman dancing held each other so closely. Exciting new dances in the 20th century were based partly on African-American and Irish traditions, like jazz and tap. In the 1920s, while dramatic Russian ballets toured Europe, ordinary people in the USA were dancing the popular and high-kicking Charleston.

YOUTH MOVEMENTS

Jitterbugging, made popular by American GI soldiers, became the fashion in the 1930s and 1940s, and developed into the sensational rock'n'roll jive of the 1940s and 1950s. The twist was a popular dance in the 1960s, and the latter part of the last century was marked by disco, breakdancing and free expression.

▶ In the popular Japanese theatre of Kabuki, an all-male cast performs comic dance, drama and singing shows, often in female dress. To give a visual climax, each scene ends with a pose called the *mie*.

SEE ALSO

Africa, Custom, Music, Theatre

DEMOCRACY

Democracy is a form of government in which the people take part in ruling the state. The people may rule directly or through elected officials.

◄ Two metal voting discs were given to each man in ancient Athens. They were used in criminal trials to vote guilty or not guilty.

People who live in a democracy either vote for officials who make laws for them, or they vote directly on laws in a meeting known as an assembly. Democracy allows people freedom of speech and the right to choose between competing political parties in regularly held elections.

◄ In some elections today, a person votes by making a mark against the candidate's name on a ballot paper. The papers (votes) are posted in a sealed ballot box, to be counted later.

POWER TO THE PEOPLE
The first democracy appeared in Ancient Greece in the 6th century BC, when men in cities could vote in assemblies. The word democracy is Greek for 'people-power'.

ELECTION VICTORY
India is the world's largest democracy and election time plays an important part in the life of the people. Candidates make speeches, distribute leaflets, advertise and design posters to persuade people to vote for them. Most candidates belong to a political party whose members share the same ideas about how the country should be run.

ELECTED ASSEMBLIES
The reign of Alexander the Great and a succession of Roman emperors gradually put an end to democracy, and the Middle Ages saw the rise of feudalism and monarchy. Democracy reappeared in the 17th century, when elected assemblies, known as parliaments, began to take power in some countries. At first only wealthy men could vote but today nearly every adult in a democracy is allowed to vote.

MAJORITY RULE
Voters choose people to represent them in legislatures (law-making bodies), such as the British House of Commons or the US Congress. For a new law to be passed, a majority in the legislature must vote for it. On important issues, there may be a vote of all the people, known as a referendum.

CHOOSING REPRESENTATIVES
Some elections are decided by a 'first past the post' system: the candidate with the most votes wins. Others are decided by proportional representation: each party gets candidates in parliament in relation to the number of votes it receives.

GOVERNMENTS AND THE LAW
There are many kinds of democracy. In Britain, there is a monarchy, but an elected parliament makes laws. France is a republic with a president and prime minister, as well as a legislature. Russia is becoming more democratic after the fall of its communist government.

SEE ALSO

Civil rights, Government, Greece (Ancient), Law, Politics

DESERT

Deserts are dry areas of land with relatively few plants or animals. Most deserts are hot, get very little rain, and are sandy or rocky.

▲ Deserts are not always hot. Some places in Antarctica and Greenland are known as polar deserts because the ground there is so dry. For example, on the western side of Antarctica, there are areas that receive less than 13cm of snow each year.

More than a fifth of the world's land surface is so dry that it is known as desert. Most deserts receive less than 250mm of rain each year. Others receive more rain than this but it evaporates quickly in the strong heat and winds, or sinks into the parched ground. The driest place in the world is the Atacama Desert in Chile, parts of which have less than 0.1mm of rain each year.

WHERE DESERTS FORM
Most deserts, such as the Kalahari and Sahara in Africa, lie between the tropics of Cancer and Capricorn (25° to the north and south of the Equator). The air in the tropics is often too hot and dry for rain clouds to form. The cold Gobi Desert in central Asia exists, however, because it is far from the sea's moist winds. Other deserts, such as the Atacama, lie behind high mountains which block the rain-bearing winds.

SURVIVAL TACTICS
Desert plants and animals have developed ways of coping with the lack of water. Plants usually have long, spreading roots to reach any available moisture. Most have spines or small leaves that are rolled or waxy to cut down on water loss through evaporation. Other plants spend most of their lives as seeds – only growing when rain falls. Desert animals often hide during the heat of the day and come out at night. Camels can go for many days without water.

POCKETS OF WATER
Oases are pockets of fertile land in a desert. These occur where an aquifer, or underground stream, comes to the surface. Plants such as palm trees thrive, and animals and people gather there.

CREEPING DESERTS
Deserts can spread. This may happen because the climate becomes drier or nearby land is overgrazed by farm animals.

IN THE SHADOW OF THE SIERRA NEVADA
The deserts of North America are shielded from rain by the towering mountain wall of the Sierra Nevada. In some areas, less than 100mm of rain falls, making the gravelly ground inhospitable except to a few plants and animals. Temperatures during the day can reach 100°C, but at night it is often near freezing because there is no cloud cover.

With its shallow, wide-ranging roots, the saguaro cactus always finds water —

Some honeypot ants fill themselves with liquid, and act as reservoirs for the rest of the nest

Scaly skin stops the rattlesnake from drying out

The kit fox sleeps in a cool burrow during the day

The roadrunner gets most of its water from the animals it catches

The prickly pear cactus stores water in its fleshy stem

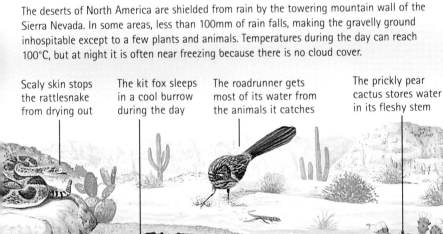

SEE ALSO
Africa, Antarctica, Climate, Habitat, Plant, South America

DESIGN

Everything we use today, from a toothbrush to a car, has been designed according to its function, to trends in fashion and art and the latest available materials.

Spanish painter Salvador Dali designed this 'Eye of Time' watch.

Even household appliances, such as the kettle, are always being re-designed.

Scottish designer and architect Charles Rennie Mackintosh designed all his chairs with unusually high backs.

Professional designers must create an object that does the job it is supposed to do as efficiently as possible. But they must also think carefully about the aesthetic value, or appearance, of the object, how and where it will be used, who will be using it, and changing trends in technology and materials.

AGE OF DESIGN
The word design comes from the Italian word *disegno*. Between the 14th and 16th centuries, during the great Italian artistic era called the Renaissance, the word was used to describe the basic idea behind a work of art, as well as rough sketches of it. Today, the term covers a huge area from detailed drawings and engineering plans for buildings to the graphic design of books, magazines and product wrappers.

SKETCHING IT OUT
The first step for many designers, whether painters, architects, film set designers or fashion designers, is to sketch out their

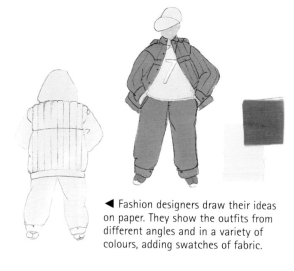

◀ Fashion designers draw their ideas on paper. They show the outfits from different angles and in a variety of colours, adding swatches of fabric.

ideas, or create storyboards on paper. If it is a building or product, they may then make up a small model to scale. Fashion designers often make up a sample garment, using inexpensive cloth.

DESIGNING ON COMPUTERS
Computers are now used extensively in design, especially for industry. They allow people to experiment with three-dimensional, often animated, models on the screen. Using CAD (Computer Aided Design), a designer can quickly change a detail and the computer will calculate and apply the changes to the rest of the design. Specialist programs help experts create cars, shoes and electrical goods.

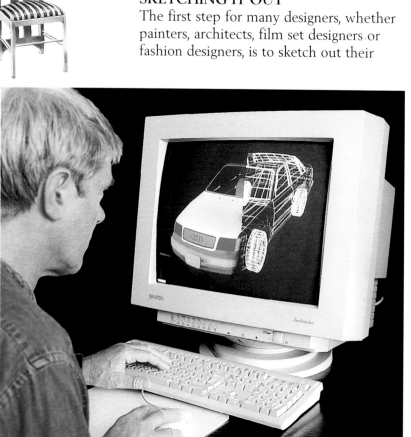

THE CREATIVE PROCESS
Computers can be used to highlight stress points, illustrate aerodynamics and show other crucial design features of a prototype car. Newspapers and magazines are designed on computer and sent to the printer on a disk, as was this book.

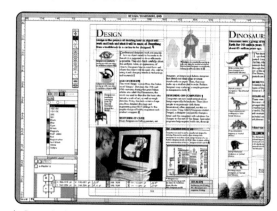

▲ Page design has been revolutionized by desktop publishing software, which allows changes to be made in seconds.

SEE ALSO
Architecture, Art, Clothing, Computer

DINOSAUR

Dinosaurs were a group of reptiles that lived on Earth for over 160 million years. They became extinct about 65 million years ago.

Tyrannosaurus rex was a theropod, or 'beast-footed' dinosaur.

Diplodocus was a sauropod, or 'lizard-footed' dinosaur.

Camptosaurus was an ornithopod, or 'bird-footed' dinosaur.

Stegosaurus was a stegosaur, or 'roofed' dinosaur.

Sauropelta was an ankylosaur, or 'jointed' dinosaur.

Triceratops was a ceratopsian, or 'horned head' dinosaur.

The dinosaurs evolved 225 million years ago during a geological period known as the Triassic. Some were only the size of a chicken, others were the biggest land animals that ever existed. They roamed the planet throughout the Jurassic period and died out at the end of the Cretaceous period. The Triassic, Jurassic and Cretaceous periods are known as the 'age of reptiles'.

MORE TO COME
The same dinosaurs did not exist throughout the 'age of reptiles'. For example, *Diplodocus* lived during the Jurassic, and *Tyrannosaurus* reigned in the Cretaceous period. Scientists have found evidence of over 500 types of dinosaur, spanning all the periods, but it is believed that as many as 1,300 types may have existed – most of which are still undiscovered.

LIZARD OR BIRD-LIKE
There were two main groups, or orders, of dinosaur – the Saurischia (with hip bones arranged like a lizard's) and the Ornithischia (with hip bones arranged like

a bird's). The Saurischia can be divided into two smaller groups known as the theropods and the sauropods. The Ornithischia include four groups: the ornithopods, the stegosaurs, the ankylosaurs and the ceratopsians.

MEAT-EATERS
The theropods were meat-eaters, all built to the same design. They had long mouths full of meat-tearing teeth, they walked on their hind legs, and had small bodies which they balanced with long, heavy tails. Some, such as *Compsognathus*, were chicken-sized, while the biggest were 12m-long killers, such as *Tyrannosaurus*. ▶

KILLING MACHINE
The theropods were the meat-eating dinosaurs, which all had large jaws full of teeth for tearing flesh. *Deinonychus* was a terrifying killing machine equipped with deadly tools, including a slashing claw on the second toe of its back foot which gave it its name – 'terrible claw'.

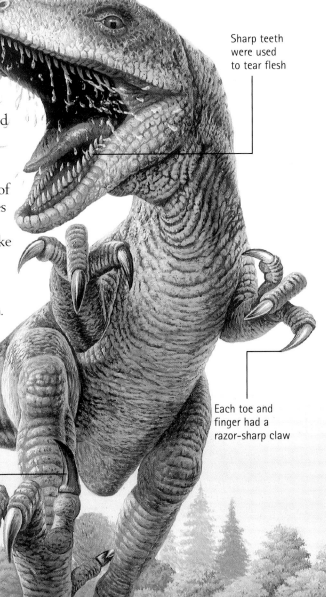

Sharp teeth were used to tear flesh

Each toe and finger had a razor-sharp claw

The second toe of its back foot had a 'terrible claw'

DINOSAUR GIANTS

Sauropods were plant-eaters. They had big, heavy bodies and moved around on all fours, using their long necks to reach leaves on trees. They were the biggest land animals that ever lived and included *Diplodocus* and *Brachiosaurus*.

CHEEKY PLANT-EATERS

The Ornithischia dinosaurs were also all plant-eaters. The only ones that could walk on their hind legs were the ornithopods. They had a more sophisticated chewing system than the long-necked sauropods, with cheeks for holding the food while they chewed it. *Iguanodon* is probably the most famous of the ornithopods.

▲ A comparison between the size of mighty *Tyrannosaurus's* feet and those of an average man.

▼ This fossil skeleton of *Tuojiangosaurus* was discovered in China in the 1970s. *Tuojiangosaurus* was a stegosaur that lived in the late Jurassic period, about 150 million years ago.

▲ In 1978, a fossilized nest of 15 young *Maiasaura* was found in Montana, USA. Evidence showed that the young were very small and would have had to be cared for by the mother to survive. *Maiasaura* means 'good mother lizard'.

BONY ARMOUR

Three ornithischian groups evolved from the ornithopods (bird-footed dinosaurs). They all had armour of some kind, which made them heavy and so they walked on four legs. The first were the stegosaurs – the 'roofed' dinosaurs. They had big bodies and either a double row of bony plates down the back like *Stegosaurus*, or an arrangement of spines like *Kentrosaurus*.

A SCENE FROM THE LATE JURASSIC

The late Jurassic is the period from 157–145 million years ago. It is known for its many plant-eating dinosaur species, such as spiny *Stegosaurus* and long-necked sauropods, including *Apatosaurus*. The main dinosaur predator was the meat-eating *Allosaurus* – although the reptile *Diplosaurus*, an ancestor of today's crocodile, was pretty fearsome.

Archaeopteryx – one of the first birds

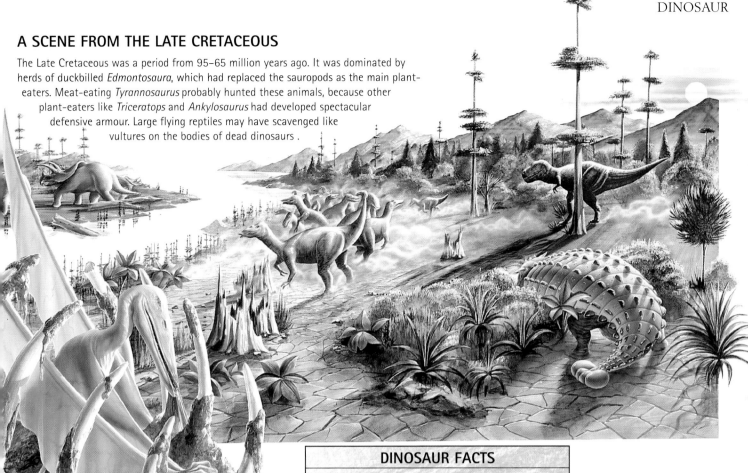

A SCENE FROM THE LATE CRETACEOUS

The Late Cretaceous was a period from 95–65 million years ago. It was dominated by herds of duckbilled *Edmontosaura*, which had replaced the sauropods as the main plant-eaters. Meat-eating *Tyrannosaurus* probably hunted these animals, because other plant-eaters like *Triceratops* and *Ankylosaurus* had developed spectacular defensive armour. Large flying reptiles may have scavenged like vultures on the bodies of dead dinosaurs .

JOINTED DINOSAURS

The second ornithischian group was the ankylosaurs, or 'jointed' dinosaurs. They had bony armour that lay flat over their broad backs, and were also armed with spikes along the sides, as in *Edmontonia*, or a tail with a club, as in *Euoplocephalus*.

HORNED HEADS

The last ornithischian group was the ceratopsians. They had armour on their faces and heads, where it formed big bony frills around the neck. These 'horned head' dinosaurs included *Triceratops*, which had a small horn on the nose and two long horns over the eyes, and *Styracosaurus*, which had an enormous horn on the nose and a series of smaller horns around the frill.

REPTILE NEIGHBOURS

Dinosaurs were not the only reptiles that lived at the time. Many groups of swimming reptiles, such as the fish-shaped ichthyosaurs and the long-necked plesiosaurs, lived in the sea, while pterosaurs flew in the air.

DINOSAUR FACTS

- The smaller meat-eating dinosaurs hunted in packs like wolves, preying on young or weak plant-eaters

- Large plant-eating dinosaurs like Diplodocus must have had to eat continuously to avoid starvation

- Dinosaurs may have been warm-blooded like mammals and birds

- Many different types of insect and mammal also lived during the time of the dinosaurs

- The dinosaurs' legs were not at the side like reptiles, but under their bodies like mammals

DEATH OF THE REPTILES

All these unusual reptiles became extinct along with the dinosaurs at the end of the Cretaceous period. Nobody knows for sure how this happened, or why other reptiles, such as crocodiles and turtles, survived. It may have been a gradual process, due to a slow climatic change, or there may have been a sudden catastrophe, such as the Earth being hit by a gigantic meteorite. The dinosaurs did leave some relatives, however. During the Jurassic period, birds evolved from the small meat-eating theropods, which means today's birds are the direct descendants of the dinosaurs.

Male

Female

▲ *Parasaurolophus* had a hollow crest extending upwards from its nose, through which it may have hooted a warning or called its mate.

SEE ALSO

Evolution, Fossil, Mammal, Prehistoric animal, Reptile

DISEASE

A disease is an illness which disturbs the normal healthy functioning of a plant, animal or person. Each disease produces symptoms (physical changes).

The human body may be attacked by thousands of diseases. These range from relatively harmless ones, such as the common cold and athlete's foot, to life-threatening diseases, such as typhoid and some cancers. Plants and animals also suffer from diseases – potatoes suffer from blight and cats can get the flu (influenza).

▲ Many diseases have almost been wiped out by the widespread use of inoculation (also called immunization and vaccination). This is when a milder form of the disease is introduced into the body, by injection or via the mouth, so that the person develops long-term resistance to the disease.

VIRUSES AND BACTERIA
Flu, AIDS and tetanus are all types of infectious disease. They are caused by harmful microscopic organisms called germs, which invade the body and multiply. Tetanus is caused by bacteria (living creatures), while flu and AIDS are caused by viruses (bundles of DNA wrapped in protein). Infectious diseases are spread from person to person by, for example, breathing in germs. A sudden outbreak of an infectious disease which affects many people is called an epidemic.

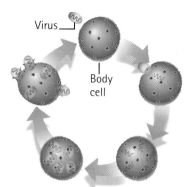

Virus

Body cell

VIRUS ATTACK
A virus spreads in the body by using the body's cells to make copies of itself. As the replicas break out, they destroy the body's cell, and each virus starts the process again.

Some infectious diseases can be prevented with vaccinations, and others can be treated with medicines such as antibiotics.

NON-INFECTIOUS DISEASES
Many diseases are not caused by germs, but are the result of poor diet. An example of this is scurvy, which is the result of not eating enough vitamin C. Others may be caused by an unhealthy lifestyle. For example, smoking and stress can lead to heart disease. Some diseases, such as haemophilia, run in families as a result of faulty genes.

LOOKING FOR CLUES
Symptoms such as pain or fever tell the person suffering from a disease that something is wrong and give clues to doctors as to the cause. A doctor can also detect signs of disease by taking X-rays or blood tests.

AFRICAN SLEEPING SICKNESS

The tsetse fly spreads a disease called sleeping sickness in some areas of Africa. When it feeds on human blood, this tiny fly injects some of its saliva into the person's bloodstream. If its saliva contains micro-organisms called *Trypanosoma brucei*, these also enter the bloodstream, and multiply inside the body, causing fever, headaches and sleepiness. The person may die if not treated quickly.

Actual size of the tsetse fly

Tsetse fly

Trypanosoma brucei

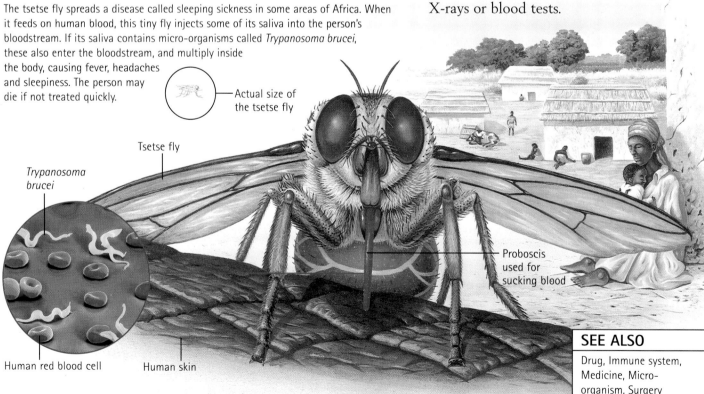

Proboscis used for sucking blood

Human red blood cell

Human skin

SEE ALSO

Drug, Immune system, Medicine, Micro-organism, Surgery

DOG

The domestic dog (*Canis familiaris*) belongs to the dog family, known as Canidae, and is believed to be descended from the grey wolf.

The chihuahua is the smallest dog in the world: only 15cm to the shoulder.

The poodle is an intelligent dog, used for finding truffles (fungi) in France.

The greyhound, bred for speed, can easily reach 57km per hour.

The bulldog was originally bred for the 'sport' of bull-baiting in the Middle Ages.

The husky is a powerful sledge dog, able to pull twice its own weight.

The Airedale is the largest breed of terrier, probably bred for hunting otters.

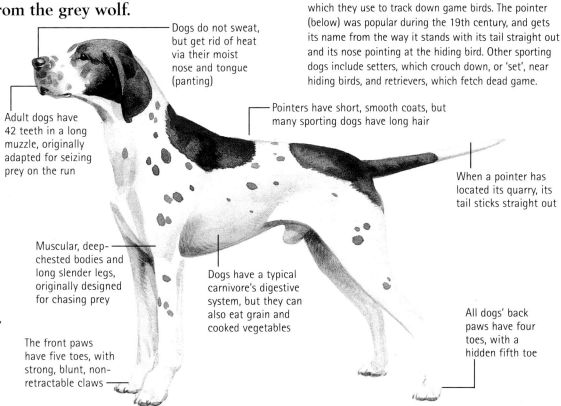

Dogs do not sweat, but get rid of heat via their moist nose and tongue (panting)

Adult dogs have 42 teeth in a long muzzle, originally adapted for seizing prey on the run

Muscular, deep-chested bodies and long slender legs, originally designed for chasing prey

The front paws have five toes, with strong, blunt, non-retractable claws

Dogs have a typical carnivore's digestive system, but they can also eat grain and cooked vegetables

Pointers have short, smooth coats, but many sporting dogs have long hair

When a pointer has located its quarry, its tail sticks straight out

All dogs' back paws have four toes, with a hidden fifth toe

SPORTING DOGS

Sporting dogs are bred for their acute sense of smell, which they use to track down game birds. The pointer (below) was popular during the 19th century, and gets its name from the way it stands with its tail straight out and its nose pointing at the hiding bird. Other sporting dogs include setters, which crouch down, or 'set', near hiding birds, and retrievers, which fetch dead game.

Dogs were the first animals to be tamed. Fossil remains of a domestic dog dating back to 10,500 years ago have been found in Idaho, USA. The relationship between human and dog probably began because dogs are natural scavengers, and hung around camps looking for food scraps.

BREEDS AND GROUPS

Since then, humans have selectively bred dogs – the American Kennel Club (AKC) recognizes 138 breeds of dog, and the British Kennel Club includes about 170. These breeds are divided into seven groups by appearance, use and size: Sporting dogs, Herding dogs, Hounds, Non-sporting dogs, Terriers, Toy dogs and Working dogs. The dog's most acute senses – smell and hearing – were selectively bred early on for guarding and hunting. Other physical features were bred for specific uses. For example, the dachshund's short legs were selected for going down badger sets, and the bulldog's set-back nose was selected to help it breathe while biting. Nowadays, a gentle, non-aggressive nature is selected for pets.

A DOG'S LIFE

Most domestic dogs are fully grown by the age of two, are old by the age of 12, and rarely live past 20. Bitches (females) can become pregnant from about seven months, and give birth to an average of three to six puppies, although some breeds may have up to ten puppies. The puppies open their eyes on the tenth day and are ready to leave their mother at six weeks. Dogs are pack animals and follow a leader. This loyalty can be transferred to a human master, especially if the dog is trained while young.

▲ The border collie uses the hunting instincts of its wild ancestors to round up sheep.

SEE ALSO

Hearing, Mammal, Wolf

DRUG

Drugs are substances that affect the way in which the body or mind works. Most drugs are used medicinally, to cure or prevent an illness.

Medicinal liquids called syrups make swallowing drugs easy for children.

Tablets and capsules are the most common form of drugs.

A drug is injected into the blood when a quick response is needed.

Eye drops and inhalers act fast by sending the drug to the exact spot.

Creams and gels often contain drugs which disinfect a cut or graze.

Skin patches release drugs slowly through the skin into the blood.

Cigarettes are made from tobacco leaves, which contain the drug nicotine.

Over 4,000 years ago, Emperor Chi'en Nung of China put together a book of more than 300 medicinal plants, many of which are still used in medicine today. But it was not until the 18th century, when the English doctor William Withering studied the heart drug digitalis (extracted from foxgloves), that drugs were looked at scientifically. The modern drug industry began in 1899, when the German company Bayer manufactured the painkiller aspirin.

TYPES OF DRUG

Doctors use many types of drug to treat patients. For example, antibiotics such as penicillin kill the bacteria that cause infections. Analgesics (painkillers), such as aspirin and codeine, stop pain messages from reaching the brain. Sedatives have a calming effect and can help a person to sleep. Anaesthetics deaden the body's nerves and are used in operations. Vaccines help the immune system to fight diseases, and insulin is given when the body fails to make enough naturally.

▶ The foxglove is listed in the oldest surviving book on drugs and their uses, written between AD20 and AD70 by the Ancient Greek doctor Dioscorides.

DANGERS AND ADDICTION

Some drugs, such as heroin or cocaine, are addictive, which means people cannot stop taking them. They are illegal because they are so dangerous. Even medicinal drugs or everyday drugs, such as alcohol, caffeine in tea and coffee or nicotine in cigarettes, can be harmful if taken in large amounts.

SLOW-RELEASE CAPSULES

Drugs sometimes need to be released into the bloodstream slowly over a few hours, especially if they are painkillers. Slow-release capsules contain hundreds of tiny pellets with coatings of different thicknesses. Some of the pellets release the drug in the stomach, while others release it later in the intestines.

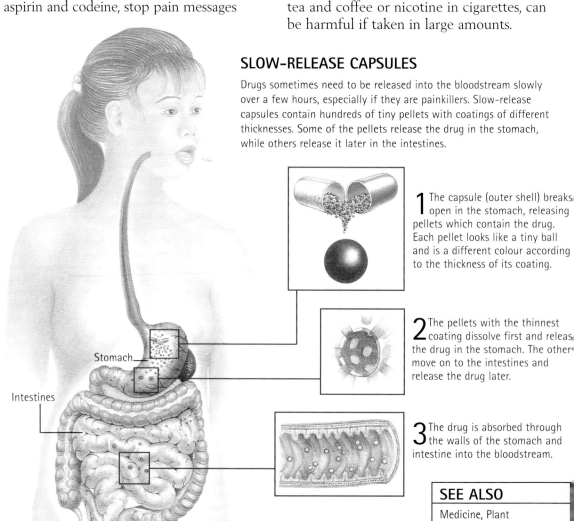

Stomach

Intestines

1 The capsule (outer shell) breaks open in the stomach, releasing pellets which contain the drug. Each pellet looks like a tiny ball and is a different colour according to the thickness of its coating.

2 The pellets with the thinnest coating dissolve first and release the drug in the stomach. The others move on to the intestines and release the drug later.

3 The drug is absorbed through the walls of the stomach and intestine into the bloodstream.

SEE ALSO
Medicine, Plant

EAGLE AND OTHER BIRDS OF PREY

Eagles and other birds of prey survive by hunting other animals. They swoop on their prey from the air, grabbing them with their sharp talons.

▶ Unlike hawks and eagles, owls, such as this Little Owl, hunt their prey at night.

Birds of prey are born hunters. They have sharp eyesight to spot far-off prey, sharp, curved talons to catch their food and strong, hooked beaks to tear at flesh. Most have large, broad wings with flight feathers that spread out when they soar in updrafts. As well as eagles, birds of prey include buzzards, falcons, hawks, kites, ospreys and vultures. Owls are also often included, but belong to a different bird group.

The Andean condor is the largest bird of prey. It can weigh up to 12kg.

HUNTING SKILLS
Most birds of prey soar high into the air and then swoop down on their prey on the ground at high speed. Some, such as the peregrine falcon, can also attack birds in mid-air. The kestrel is unusual because it hovers just a few metres above the ground before swooping. Vultures usually scavenge dead meat.

When peregrine falcons dive, they can reach speeds of over 250km/h.

DIFFERENT TASTES
There are more than 50 species of eagle scattered throughout the world, although many are endangered. Most live in wild, remote places where humans cannot disturb them. Eagles eat a wide range of animals. The golden eagle attacks hares, small rodents and other birds, while the bateleur eagle gorges on snakes. Some are experts at snaring fish, and the harpy eagle catches monkeys.

Northern goshawks can strike in mid-air, often attacking from below.

FISH FOR DINNER
The bald eagle, the national bird of the USA, is one of the most endangered birds of prey. It feeds on birds and small animals, but particularly likes fish. It scoops them from the surface of the water and flies off, gripping them in its sharp talons.

Vultures, such as this black vulture, feed on the bodies of dead animals.

The golden eagle is the most widespread eagle in the Northern Hemisphere.

NEST RECYCLING
Many eagles use the same nest, or eyrie, again and again, adding more material each time they breed. Their nests can become enormous – a bald eagle's can measure 3m across and weigh over a tonne. Most eagles lay just two eggs. Once the young have hatched, they do not leave the nest for up to two months.

SEE ALSO
Bird

EARTH

Our planet, Earth, is one of the nine planets that move around the Sun. It is made up of rock and metal, and is the only planet known to support life.

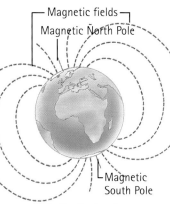

▲ As the Earth spins, electrical currents beneath the surface turn the planet into a huge magnet, with a north and south pole just like any ordinary magnet.

Planet Earth is an almost perfect ball of rock with a metal core, which travels around the Sun. It is surrounded by a blanket of gases called the atmosphere, has one moon, and as far as we know, is the only planet that supports life.

NIGHT AND DAY

Approximately every 24 hours, the Earth does a full circle on its axis – an imaginary line joining the North and South Poles. As it spins, one side turns to face the Sun and is in daylight, while the other side turns away, experiencing night. The Earth spins eastward, which is why the Sun seems to rise in the east and set in the west.

AROUND THE SUN

As well as spinning on its own axis, the Earth is constantly moving around the Sun. One complete path around the Sun is an orbit. The length of a year is determined by the time it takes a planet to make one orbit. This means that the Earth travels 958 million kilometres at an average speed of 30km per second.

CHANGING SEASONS

The Earth is tilted towards the Sun at an angle of 23.5°. As the Earth orbits, those places that are tilted towards the Sun receive more warmth and light for the part of the year that is known as summer. As these places move further round, they tilt away from the Sun, experiencing winter.

THE EARTH'S MAKE-UP

Beneath its thin shell, or crust, the interior of the Earth is very hot. Below about 70km, there is a mantle of rock that is semi-molten (partly melted). The outer layer of the Earth's core is molten too, but enormous pressure keeps the inner core (the centre) solid, even though temperatures here reach over 6,000°C. The upper layer of the mantle is made of plates, like pieces of a jigsaw, with the continents on top. Sometimes, the plates rub together, causing pressure which escapes via volcanoes or earthquakes.

FROM CORE TO CRUST

If we could cut a piece out of the Earth like a giant apple, we would see a planet made in four layers. At its centre is a solid inner core of almost pure iron, surrounded by an outer core of liquid iron and nickel. Enveloping this is a mantle of silicon compounds, crystals and lighter metals, topped with a hard rock crust.

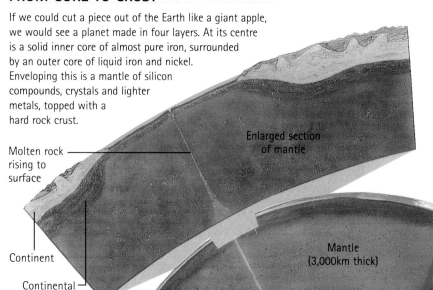

Enlarged section of mantle

Molten rock rising to surface

Continent

Continental plate

Mantle (3,000km thick)

Outer core (2,200km thick)

Inner core (2,500km across)

The Earth is wrapped in a blanket of gases known as the atmosphere, which stretches up more than 500km into space. It is held in place by the gravitational pull of the planet

THE EVOLVING EARTH

Astronomers believe that the Earth began to form about 4.6 billion years ago, when the solar nebula (a vast cloud of hot debris circling the newly formed Sun) began to cluster together into lumps that eventually became the planets of our solar system. The process took millions of years to complete and Earth, like the other planets, developed a unique chemistry and atmosphere.

1 Hot clouds of dust and gases spin around the newly formed Sun. As the specks of dust collide, they stick together in lumps.

2 The forces of gravity pull more passing lumps into the spinning ball. Heavy elements such as iron sink to the centre.

3 Lighter metals and rocks come to the surface and the red-hot Earth cools enough for a hard shell to form.

4 Gases escaping from the Earth form clouds and rain falls, creating oceans containing small oxygen-producing plants.

5 Originally one large mass of land, the Earth's land surface is now split into seven chunks, known as continents.

LIFE ON EARTH

Why exactly there is life on Earth is still a mystery to scientists. The theories are numerous, but the answer is probably a combination of reasons. Firstly, Earth's distance from the Sun is ideal – not too hot like Venus, nor too cold like Mars. Secondly, Earth is the only planet we know of that has water on its surface – over 70 per cent of it is covered by water. Scientists believe that electrical storms on the newly formed planet caused chemical reactions between gases in the atmosphere. these created the first building blocks of life, which fell into the oceans, where they combined to form simple plant-like creatures. All plants make oxygen, and so an ideal atmosphere was soon created for the evolution of oxygen-breathing life forms.

Earth

Moon

▲ A day is the time it takes the Earth to turn once on its own axis: 23 hours, 56 minutes and 4 seconds.

▲ A lunar month is the time it takes the Moon to travel once around the Earth: 28 days.

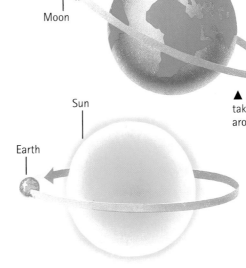

Sun

Earth

▲ A year is the time it takes the Earth to travel once around the Sun: 365 days, 6 hours and 9 minutes.

EARTH FACTS AND FIGURES

• The Earth's diameter (the distance from Pole to Pole through the centre) is 12,714km

• The Earth's circumference (the distance around its middle at the Equator) is 40,075km

• As the Earth spins, places near the Equator move much faster than places at the Poles, causing the planet to bulge slightly in the middle and be flattened at the top and bottom

• The temperature of the Earth's inner core may be as hot as 6,200°C

• Of the nine planets in our solar system, Earth is the third closest to the Sun

• The Sun and the Earth are about 150 million kilometres apart

• The Earth's path around the Sun is not a circle but an ellipse (an oval), which means it is closer to the Sun on January 1 than on June 1

SEE ALSO

Atmosphere, Big Bang theory, Continent, Earthquake, Evolution, Gravity, Magnetism, Planet, Season, Solar system, Sun, Time, Volcano

EARTHQUAKE

An earthquake is a shaking of the Earth's surface. It is caused by the sudden release of pressure through weak parts of the Earth's crust.

The vast majority of earthquakes do not cause any serious damage. Small tremors can happen with an erupting volcano, an avalanche or a landslide. However, the largest earthquakes occur as a result of pressure or tension deep under the ground being released through weak areas (fault lines) in the Earth's crust.

TECTONIC PLATES

The Earth's crust is broken into giant slabs called tectonic plates. Sometimes, pressure builds up underground as a result of the plates moving against each other. The pressure is suddenly released, sending out shock waves in all directions and causing the Earth's crust to shake and even crack.

EARTHQUAKE ZONES

Two great earthquake zones exist. Both are where two tectonic plates meet. One stretches across southern Asia, through the Mediterranean and into East Africa. The other is the 'ring of fire' around the Pacific Ocean, which includes the USA. In 1906, a large part of San Francisco was destroyed by an earthquake in this zone.

Fault line

Epicentre

Hypocentre

Shock waves

▲ The shock waves begin underground in a region called the hypocentre and reach the Earth's surface directly above, at the epicentre. From here, they radiate out in all directions.

SHOCK WAVES

Earthquake shock waves are known as seismic waves. They are detected using a measuring instrument called a seismometer. A severe earthquake can be felt as much as 400km away. The intensity of an earthquake is plotted on the Richter scale. An earthquake measuring over 7 on this scale can destroy buildings and take lives.

DISASTER IN JAPAN

In 1995, the Japanese city of Kobe was devastated by a violent earthquake that killed over 5,000 people. The earthquake measured 7.2 on the Richter scale. It caused houses and apartments to collapse, trains to be derailed and roads to be ripped apart. The shaking lasted for about 20 seconds.

SEE ALSO

Continent, Earth, Mountain and valley, Ocean and sea, Volcano

EASTERN EUROPE

Eastern Europe is a geographical region of eight countries that were once part of the communist bloc controlled by the Soviet Union.

BELARUS
Area: 207,600 sq km
Population: 10,335,382
Capital: Minsk
Languages: Belarusian and Russian
Currency: Rouble

CZECH REPUBLIC
Area: 78,866 sq km
Population: 10,256,760
Capital: Prague
Language: Czech
Currency: Koruna

HUNGARY
Area: 93,030 sq km
Population: 10,075,034
Capital: Budapest
Language: Hungarian
Currency: Forint

MOLDOVA
Area: 33,843 sq km
Population: 4,434,547
Capital: Chisinau
Language: Moldovan
Currency: Leu

POLAND
Area: 312,685 sq km
Population: 38,625,478
Capital: Warsaw
Language: Polish
Currency: Zloty

Eastern Europe lies between the Baltic Sea, the Balkan peninsula, the Black Sea and Russia. It makes up more than one sixth of Europe's land area, and is a region of plains, low hills and mountains.

PEAKS AND PLAINS
To the south lie the rugged Carpathian Mountains and Transylvanian Alps. The highest point is Gerlachovsky Stit, a peak of 2,656m in the Carpathians. To the west is the Hungarian Plain and to the east are the vast rolling steppes (grasslands) of Ukraine.

A REGION OF RIVERS
The area is watered by some of Europe's major rivers. The Danube, Europe's second longest river (2,858km), forms much of Romania's southwestern border, while the Dnieper and the Dniester both flow through Ukraine. Europe's largest swamp, the Pripet Marshes, straddles the border between Belarus and Ukraine.

▲ Huge expanses of steppe once covered Ukraine but this land, covered with rich soil, is now heavily farmed.

CONTINENTAL CLIMATE
Away from the mountains, Eastern Europe has warm summers with average temperatures reaching 20°C or more in July. Winters get colder as you travel from west to east. Most of the region has moderate rainfall, with 500mm to 1,000mm per year, but the southeast is drier, with less than 500mm of rain a year.

BREAD BASKET OF EUROPE
In the lowlands, many of the region's forests have been cleared for farming. The fertile steppes, once an area of natural grassland, are also farmed. Ukraine is sometimes called 'the bread basket of Europe' because of its high production of grains and other crops. ▶

▼ The medieval city of Prague, capital of the Czech Republic, has some of Europe's most beautiful and well-preserved architecture.

N

BALTIC SEA

miles
0   100
0   100
km

LATVIA

LITHUANIA

RUSSIA

■Minsk

BELARUS

RUSSIA

GERMANY

Vistula

Warsaw ■

POLAND

Pripet
Marshes

Prague ■

CZECH REPUBLIC

Kiev ■

UKRAINE

Dnieper

▲
Gerlachovsky
Stit

Dniester

SLOVAKIA

Carpathian

MOLDOVA

■Bratislava

AUSTRIA

Mountains

Chisinau ■

HUNGARY

■Budapest

Danube

Hungarian Plain

CASPIAN
SEA

SLOVENIA

ROMANIA

BLACK
SEA

CROATIA

Transylvanian Alps

UNION OF
SERBIA AND
MONTENEGRO

Bucharest ■

Danube

BULGARIA

BALKAN PENINSULA

ROMANIA
Area: 237,500 sq km
Population: 22,317,730
Capital: Bucharest
Language: Romanian
Currency: Leu

SLOVAKIA
Area: 48,845 sq km
Population: 5,422,366
Capital: Bratislava
Language: Slovak
Currency: Koruna

UKRAINE
Area: 603,700 sq km
Population: 48,396,470
Capital: Kiev
Language: Ukrainian
Currency: Hryvna

► Old-fashioned factories,
such as this one in
Romania, cause air, water
and soil pollution in many
parts of Eastern Europe.

DISAPPEARING WILDLIFE

As in the rest of Europe, the wildlife in
Eastern Europe has been reduced by the
destruction of forests and grasslands. A
number of large mammals that once grazed
on the steppes, such as the saiga antelope,
have now disappeared. The rare wisent
(European bison) is found in western
Belarus and central Poland, while the
Danube delta on the Black Sea is a major
wetland and home to many birds.

HEAVY AND LIGHT INDUSTRY

Coal, oil and natural gas, iron ore and
other minerals are found in this region.
Heavy industry produces machinery,

▲ The practice of Eastern Orthodox Christianity is widespread in Belarus, Moldova, Romania and Ukraine. Here, Holy Communion is celebrated in Kiev, Ukraine.

transport equipment and steel, and the manufacture of electronic goods, clothes and processed food is increasing.

CITY DWELLERS
Many people live in rural areas, and a few people still follow a nomadic lifestyle. But about two thirds of the people live and work in towns and cities. Kiev, in Ukraine, is the largest city in Eastern Europe, with a population of 2,651,000.

RELIGIOUS WORSHIP
Religion is an important part of life for many people in Eastern Europe. The two dominant faiths in the region are Roman Catholic and Eastern Orthodox Christianity. There is a Muslim minority in Romania, which was once part of the Muslim Ottoman Empire.

FOREIGN POWERS
All of the countries of Eastern Europe have at times in their history been under the influence of a foreign power. In 1793,

DEMOCRACY IN HUNGARY
From the end of World War II, Hungary, like the rest of Eastern Europe, came under Soviet communist rule. However, demonstrations in favour of democracy, such as this one in Budapest in 1988, indicated people's unhappiness with the government. In 1989, Hungary was the first Eastern European country to shake off communism. In March 1990, it elected its first democratic government in 42 years.

Poland disappeared after being divided up among Prussia, Austria and Russia. Hungary and Czechoslovakia formed part of the Habsburg Empire until 1918. Romania gained its independence from Turkey in 1878. More recently, Ukraine, Belarus and Moldova were part of the Russian-dominated Soviet Union.

COMMUNIST RULE
After World War II, all the countries of Eastern Europe came under communist rule, either as part of the Soviet Union or as members of the Soviet bloc. Romania remained outside Soviet control, but under the communist dictator Nicolae Ceausescu.

THE NEW MAP
In the late 1980s, the countries of Eastern Europe began to abandon communist rule in favour of their own democratically elected governments. Belarus, Moldova and Ukraine gained their independence in 1991, following the break-up of the Soviet Union. In 1993, Czechoslovakia split peacefully into two countries: the Czech Republic and Slovakia.

▲ Holiday-makers in Budapest play chess in one of Hungary's many natural hot springs.

EUROPA!

CAVE

CANEM

SEE ALSO
Cold War, Communism, Democracy, Europe, Russia and the Baltic States

ECOLOGY

Ecology is the study of how plants, animals and humans live together in their natural surroundings, and the ways in which they affect one another.

THE FOOD CHAIN

Each organism in a food chain feeds on and gets energy from the level above. Ecologists divide plants and animals in a chain into groups, depending on how they get their energy. Plants are energy producers, using the Sun's energy to produce new growth. Animals are consumers, obtaining energy by eating plants or other animals.

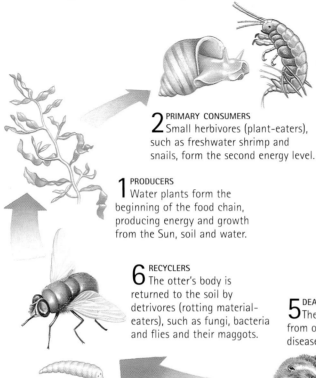

2 PRIMARY CONSUMERS
Small herbivores (plant-eaters), such as freshwater shrimp and snails, form the second energy level.

1 PRODUCERS
Water plants form the beginning of the food chain, producing energy and growth from the Sun, soil and water.

3 SECONDARY CONSUMERS
The third level of energy usage is by larger carnivores (meat-eaters) such as trout, which feed on the shrimp and snails.

6 RECYCLERS
The otter's body is returned to the soil by detrivores (rotting material-eaters), such as fungi, bacteria and flies and their maggots.

4 TOP PREDATOR
In the fourth level of energy transfer, a bigger carnivore such as an otter preys on the trout.

5 DEATH
The otter dies from old age or disease.

Every plant and animal depends on a cycle of food, energy and waste disposal that links it to other plants and animals. Ecologists study how plants and animals are linked to each other in food chains and webs.

CHAINED TOGETHER

All living things need energy. Plants use light energy from the Sun to turn substances in the soil, air and water into food. Insects eat the plants, and fish, birds and other animals eat the insects. In this way, energy is passed along a food chain. When living things die, their bodies break down and release nutrients back into the ground to start the process again.

ECOSYSTEMS

An ecosystem is made up of the plants and animals in a certain area, together with the air, soil, climate and other non-living things. A forest is one type of ecosystem, but there are many others. An ecosystem can be as small as a pond or as large as an ocean.

HUMANS INTERVENE

Humans are part of the biggest ecosystem of all – the Earth itself. Some human actions can affect the entire planet. Logging a rainforest, for example, affects the forest by destroying its plants and animals. Since trees produce the oxygen needed by humans and other life forms, the world's oxygen supply is also affected.

GREY SQUIRREL INVASION

The introduction of animals or plants from foreign lands can have harmful effects on the ecology of an area. When grey squirrels from North America were introduced to Britain, the native red squirrels were pushed out of the food chain in most areas.

▲ Many timber companies manage their forests ecologically using a process known as artificial reforestation. This means that a constant supply of seeds is sown in a nursery and transplanted to the forest to replace felled trees.

SEE ALSO

Animal, Brazil, Conservation, Forest, Habitat, Plant, Pollution

EDUCATION

Education is the development of skills and knowledge. It can be formal, as provided by schools, or informal – via playing, watching and learning in everyday life.

Learning to play a musical instrument is free as part of the curriculum in some countries. In other places, pupils must pay for lessons.

Many people feel that the main reason for educating children is to benefit society, by teaching skills needed to keep the community going. Others feel that it is more important to develop an individual's talents and interests. The Ancient Greek philosopher Socrates believed that education could make people happier.

SCHOOL FOR ALL

The Ancient Greeks were the first to set up a formal education system, but only for boys of rich families. Lessons included the art of public speaking for budding politicians. In many countries, the church or charities governed schooling. It wasn't until the 1800s that governments began to take control, and the 1900s before education became free for most girls and boys. However, millions of people worldwide still do not possess the basic skills of reading and writing.

School trips are a fun and exciting way of relating subjects learnt in the classroom to real-life objects and situations.

BEST YEARS OF YOUR LIFE

In most countries, it is compulsory for children to go to primary school at the age of five or six, then on to a secondary (high) school at about 11 years of age. Some start earlier. Friedrich Froebel opened the first kindergarten (nursery) in Germany in 1837. In many parts of the world, attendance drops after the age of 11, but education can continue into adulthood at colleges or universities. Courses offer vocational (career) training or specialist qualifications.

THE CURRICULUM

The curriculum (subjects taught) varies in each country. It may emphasize religion, local crafts or history. Many 19th-century schools concentrated on reading, writing and arithmetic. Subjects and teaching methods have changed over the years, as have educational theories. The 17th-century Czech educationalist, Comenius, thought pictures were a vital teaching tool. Italian reformer Maria Montessori (1870–1952) devised wooden apparatus to help children learn through exploration.

SCHOOLS OF THOUGHT

Styles of teaching, subjects taught and classroom settings have changed over the years. Once children had to sit in rows in silence while the teacher lectured them. Now, there is more emphasis on interaction and small group tuition. Educators argue about which is best – formal instruction (presenting facts to learn) or learning through activity and experience.

▲ A government health advisor visits a classroom in the USA in 1925 to instruct children on healthy eating.

SEE ALSO

Greece (Ancient)

EGYPT

Egypt lies in the northeast of Africa. It has more people than any other African nation except Nigeria, yet most of the people live in just four per cent of the country.

Area: 1,001,449 sq km
Population: 70,712,345
Capital: Cairo
Language: Arabic
Currency: Egyptian pound

Most Egyptians live around the Nile delta and valley, and along the Suez Canal, a vital shipping link for world trade. The River Nile, controlled by the Aswan High Dam, provides fertile land stretching from Egypt's border with Sudan in the south right up to the Mediterranean Sea in the north. Egypt's main cities are its capital, Cairo, and the port of Alexandria – two of the largest cities in Africa.

DESERT AREAS

On either side of the Nile lie two deserts that together cover more than 90 per cent of the country – the vast, low-lying Western Desert and the hilly Eastern Desert, which borders the Red Sea.

AGRICULTURAL LIFE

Agriculture is the country's most important industry, employing over a third of all Egyptians. These farmers, known as *fellahin*, grow cotton and food crops such as maize and rice in the fertile Nile delta. The manufacturing industry is growing, and tourists attracted by the ancient ruins also generate income for many Egyptians. Cotton, oil and cloth are major exports.

Traders, such as this man selling herbs and tea, set up their stalls in open street markets, or bazaars.

A MUSLIM POPULATION

Most Egyptians are descended from the people of Ancient Egypt or from Arabs who invaded in the 7th century AD. Over 90 per cent of the people are Muslims.

EGYPT TODAY

Egypt was part of the Ottoman Empire from 1517 until 1922. Britain controlled the Suez Canal and had administrative power in the country from the 1880s until the 1950s. Since the 1980s, Egypt has strengthened its ties with other Arab nations, such as Saudi Arabia.

Egypt's main port of Alexandria was the world's greatest trading city 2,000 years ago.

▶ Triangular-sailed wooden boats called feluccas carry goods and passengers along the Nile.

SEE ALSO
Africa, Egypt (Ancient), Islam, Middle East

EGYPT ANCIENT

Ancient Egypt developed along the River Nile around 5,000 years ago. Over the next 2,500 years, it grew into one of the greatest civilizations of all time.

The funeral mask of Tutankhamen, boy-king of Egypt (1361-52BC), was discovered in 1922.

The tombs of important officials contained models of items that they might need in the next world.

The Ancient Egyptians chose to settle by the Nile in Africa because each year the river flooded, spreading mud over the banks. This provided them with fertile land to farm.

PYRAMID BUILDERS

The Ancient Egyptians were the first real engineers and built impressive temples, cities and pyramids. The largest of the pyramids needed over two million blocks of stone, each weighing as much as 2.5 tonnes. Some were cut from distant quarries and floated down the Nile by raft.

IMPORTANT INVENTORS

The Egyptians used papyrus reeds to make shoes, boats, ropes and writing paper. Papyrus scrolls preserve Ancient Egyptian hieroglyphic writing. The Egyptians also invented a 365-day calendar.

▲ Pyramids were burial monuments for kings. A Sphinx (half man, half lion) stands beside the pyramids at Giza.

LIFE AFTER DEATH

Many gods were worshipped, including the sun-god Ra, and Osiris, god of the dead. The Egyptian kings, or pharaohs, were also believed to be gods. When they died, the kings and queens were buried in tombs full of things they might need in the next world – food, jewels, even small statues of servants (*shabtis*). Most royal tombs were later robbed, but in 1922, the tomb of the boy pharaoh Tutankhamen was found with most of its treasures untouched.

THREE GREAT ERAS

Ancient Egypt included three great ages: the Old Kingdom, the Middle Kingdom and the New Kingdom. In 31BC, Cleopatra died and Egypt fell to the Rome Empire.

MUMMIFIED BODIES

The Ancient Egyptians believed in life after death. Their bodies were mummified (preserved) before burial to prevent decay. It took 70 days to mummify a body.

The body was preserved in salt for 40 days to dry. Before being bandaged, the dried body was rubbed with oils and spices and the heart placed inside

Most of the internal organs were put into canopic jars. This human-headed one held the liver

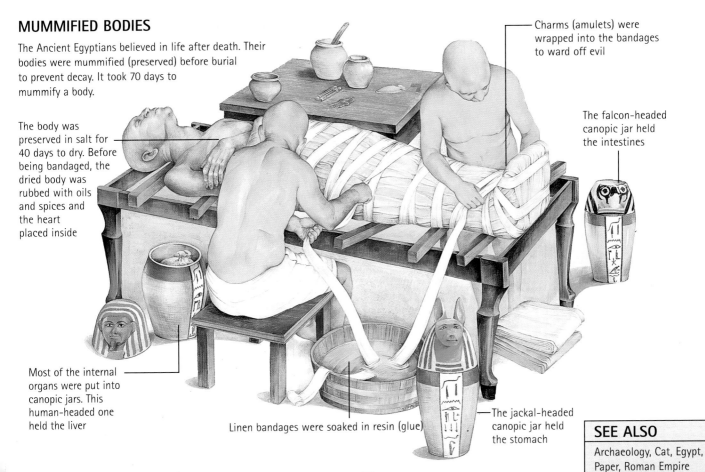

Charms (amulets) were wrapped into the bandages to ward off evil

The falcon-headed canopic jar held the intestines

Linen bandages were soaked in resin (glue)

The jackal-headed canopic jar held the stomach

SEE ALSO

Archaeology, Cat, Egypt, Paper, Roman Empire

ELECTRICITY

Electricity is a form of energy. It can be stored in batteries or sent along wires to make electric trains, computers, light bulbs and other devices work.

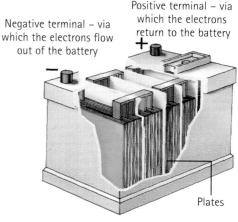

Negative terminal – via which the electrons flow out of the battery

Positive terminal – via which the electrons return to the battery

Plates

▲ Wet batteries, like those in cars, store electricity and can be recharged. Six cells contain lead and lead dioxide plates in a solution of dilute sulphuric acid. The battery is first charged by an outside electrical source, but after that a generator, run by the car's engine, keeps it charged.

Electricity is an invisible form of energy created by the movement of charged particles. It flows into our homes along wires and can be easily converted into other energy forms, such as heat and light.

▲ Each light bulb in a circuit creates resistance to the flow of electric current, and so light bulbs wired in series do not glow brightly.

PASSING ON ELECTRONS
Everything in the world, including humans and the air they breathe, is made of atoms. Each of these tiny particles has a positively charged centre (nucleus), with smaller, negatively charged electrons whizzing around it. Electricity is created when one of the electrons jumps to another atom. This can be caused by the magnetic field in a generator, by chemicals in a battery, or by friction (rubbing materials together).

THALES THE PHILOSOPHER
The discovery that an electric charge could be created by rubbing two materials together was first made by the Greek philosopher Thales over 2,600 years ago. He found that if he rubbed the fossilized tree sap, amber, with silk, it attracted feathers and dust. We now know that this happened because electrons had been passed between the silk and the amber,

▲ Light bulbs wired in parallel all glow brightly, because each light bulb is connected directly to the battery.

making them electrically charged. In recognition of his discovery, our word electron comes from the Greek word *elecktron*, meaning amber.

CONDUCTORS AND INSULATORS
The electricity of substances such as amber is called static electricity because the charge stays put once the electrons have moved between the atoms. In other substances, the electrons carry on flowing. These substances are called conductors. Most electrical wires are made of copper because it is a good electrical conductor, as are all metals. Water also conducts electricity, which is why it is dangerous to

HOW A GENERATOR WORKS
An electric generator works by using the principle of electro-magnetic induction discovered in 1831 by the British chemist and physicist Michael Faraday (1791–1867). He discovered that if a coil of wire is spun between two magnets, electrons begin to flow inside the wire coil. An alternating current (AC) and a direct current (DC) can be created in this way.

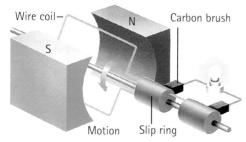

Wire coil

N

S

Carbon brush

Motion   Slip ring

▲ The two magnets naturally produce an alternating current (AC). As the coil spins, the magnetic field inside the coil points first one way and then the other. This makes the electric current change direction, or alternate.

Wire coil

Carbon brush

N

S

Commutator

Motion

▲ To create a direct current (DC), which flows in only one direction, the coil must be attached to a device called a commutator which is able to reverse the current.

▶ Practical DC generators are used to power large industrial motors. Unlike Faraday's simple model, a generator has many coils of wire wound on a rotor.

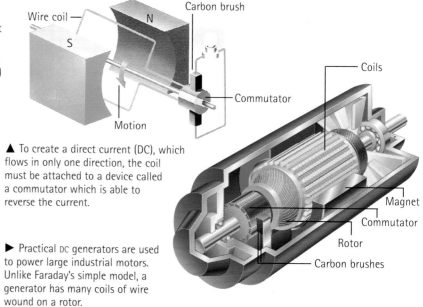

Coils

Magnet

Commutator

Rotor

Carbon brushes

ELECTRICAL TERMS

Conductor Any substance through which an electric current can flow

Coulomb (C) The measurement of electric charge

Current How fast electrons flow along a conductor – it is measured in amperes (A)

Insulator Any substance through which an electric current cannot flow

Resistance How hard it is for current to flow through a conductor – it is measured in ohms (Ω)

Static electricity Electric charge created by two objects rubbing together and exchanging electrons

Voltage (V) A unit of measurement describing how powerfully a battery sends electric current

Watt A unit of measurement that describes how much electrical energy can be converted into heat and light energy per second

operate electrical appliances with wet hands. Other materials are made of atoms between which it is almost impossible for electrons to flow. These materials are known as insulators, and include plastic, wood and amber. A flow of electrons is known as a current, and the term 'resistance' is a measure of how difficult it is for current to flow through a conductor.

COMPLETING THE CIRCUIT

For an electrical appliance such as a torch to work, its electricity source (the battery) must be connected to the bulb by wires in an unbroken loop. This is known as a circuit. The job of the torch's ON/OFF switch is to open or close a gap in the circuit. When the switch is on, electricity is allowed to flow around the circuit, lighting the bulb. When the switch is off, the circuit is broken and the current cannot flow.

MAINS SUPPLY

Batteries have a limited amount of chemicals and can only provide a certain amount of electricity. That is why most electrical devices are powered by a mains supply. Wires connect millions of wall sockets to a power station. An electric current flows from the power station along the wires, out of the sockets and into the equipment being used. To complete the circuit, the current returns to the power station through yet more wires.

PRODUCING ELECTRICITY

All power stations have a generator which produces electricity. In nuclear power stations, the nuclear reactor creates the heat needed to turn water into steam. The steam turns giant wheels, called turbines, which power the generator. The electricity it produces then flows along wires to homes, shops and offices.

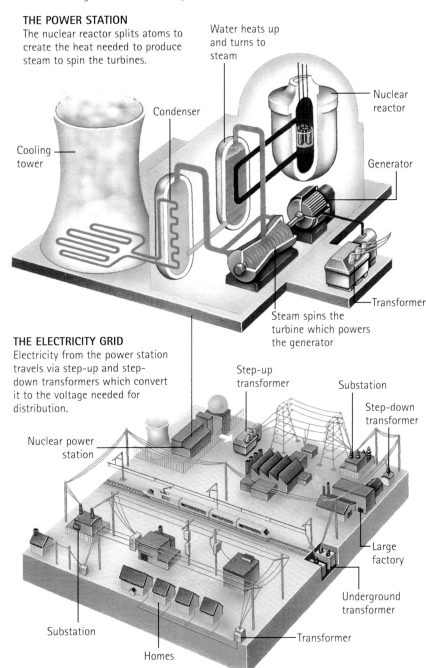

THE POWER STATION
The nuclear reactor splits atoms to create the heat needed to produce steam to spin the turbines.

Water heats up and turns to steam

Condenser

Nuclear reactor

Cooling tower

Generator

Transformer

Steam spins the turbine which powers the generator

THE ELECTRICITY GRID
Electricity from the power station travels via step-up and step-down transformers which convert it to the voltage needed for distribution.

Nuclear power station

Step-up transformer

Substation

Step-down transformer

Large factory

Underground transformer

Substation

Homes

Transformer

ALTERNATING CURRENT

The electricity that comes out of a power station is in the form of alternating current (AC). Unlike a battery, which produces a steady one-way current called a direct current (DC), the mains supply flows first in one direction and then the other. The current changes direction very rapidly (about 50 times a second).

SEE ALSO

Atom and molecule, Electronics, Energy, Heat, Magnetism, Nuclear power

ELECTRONICS

Electronics is a branch of engineering which studies the components and circuits that make up modern electrical devices, such as radios and toasters.

Until the 1950s, radios used glass valves, which were bulky and fragile.

In the 1950s, the small, robust transistor began to replace the valve.

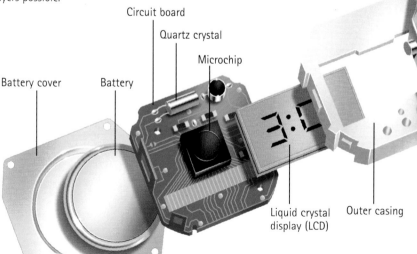

In the 1970s, microchips made hand-sized radio-cassette players possible.

Modern electrical devices contain tiny electronic parts called components, which are joined together by lines of metallic paint on circuit boards. Electronic engineers know how to put together the right components to make circuits that can perform specific jobs.

WORKING PARTS
Components affect the way electrons (tiny charged particles) flow through a circuit. The simplest component, the switch, breaks the flow of electrons, or current. Resistors make it harder for the current to flow, while capacitors store current as electrical charge. Diodes let current flow in only one direction.

TRANSISTOR TECHNOLOGY
The first circuits used bulky glass valves, or vacuum tubes, which could magnify a current or switch it on or off. This ability to turn a current on or off electronically is the principle behind all computers. In the 1950s, the valve was replaced by a device called the transistor, which was much smaller, cheaper and more durable, paving the way for the huge electronic advances that were to follow.

BIRTH OF THE MICROCHIP
In the 1970s, the invention of the microchip, which contained thousands of tiny transistors on a piece of material smaller than a stamp, enabled complex circuits to be squeezed into a tiny space. This made the home computer possible. More recently, Very Large Scale Integration (VLSI) has allowed hundreds of millions of transistors to be put on a single chip, meaning that even smaller computers can be made.

ELECTRONICS TODAY
Electronics is now part of virtually all electrical devices. The microprocessor, a complex circuit fitted onto a single chip, is used in devices ranging from space rockets and robots to video-cassette recorders, telephones and digital watches.

HOW A DIGITAL WATCH WORKS
A digital watch is powered by a battery. Its timing is controlled by a quartz crystal, which vibrates thousands of times a second. The microchip uses these vibrations to keep time, which it displays in numbers.

Battery cover

Battery

Circuit board

Quartz crystal

Microchip

Liquid crystal display (LCD)

Outer casing

Plastic window

SEE ALSO
Atom and molecule, Clock, Computer, Electricity, Robot, Rocket, Telephone

ELEPHANT

Elephants are the largest animals on land. They have very thick skin, a trunk and ivory tusks. There are two species of elephant: the African and the Asian.

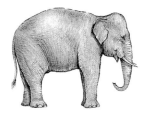

Asian elephants are the smaller type, growing to 3m at the shoulder and weighing up to 5 tonnes.

African elephants are the largest land animals. They can reach 4m and weigh up to 6 tonnes.

The African elephant lives in forests and open grassland and is the largest living land animal. The Asian or Indian elephant is mainly a forest animal. It is also smaller, with smaller ears, a more rounded back and a trunk that ends in one finger-like tip, instead of two.

EATING MACHINES

Elephants live on a diet of leaves and bark, eating up to 200kg of food a day. They use their strong trunks, which are giant, flexible nostrils, to pull up plants and to bring food and water to their mouths. They have 12 back teeth (molars), but only four are fully developed and in use at any one time. All elephants have tusks, or extra long curved teeth, which they use to strip bark off trees and to dig for water.

PROTECTIVE INSTINCTS

Female elephants start to breed when they are about ten years old. They are pregnant for 20 months, before giving birth to a single calf. When a calf is about to be born, other females gather around the mother and the herd stays in one place until the young calf, which stands nearly a metre tall, is on its feet and ready to move on.

▶ An elephant's tusks are long, curved teeth called incisors. About one third of the tusk is hidden in the skull.

Skull
Upper jaw
Lower jaw
Tusk (incisor tooth)

COOLING DOWN

Because elephants have no sweat glands, they lose very little body heat. They cool down by hiding in the shade and flapping their ears, or by bathing in water and using their trunks to shower themselves.

OLD AGE

All elephants, except the old bull males, are sociable animals and live in herds led by the oldest females. They can live for over 60 years, but many are killed for their ivory tusks. In many places the bull elephants, which have the biggest tusks, have become rare. The spread of human settlements has also led to both Asian and African elephants becoming endangered.

SEE ALSO

Africa, Animal, India, Mammal

EMPIRE

An empire is a group of nations or states under the control of a single power. Most empires are built up when one country conquers others.

Octavian, later called, Augustus, became the first Emperor of Rome in 27BC.

From 527 to 565, Justinian ruled the Byzantine Empire with his wife Theodora.

In 1525, Babar founded the Mughal Empire by conquering northern India.

Suleiman strengthened and enlarged the 16th-century Ottoman Empire.

Maria Theresa and Francis I unified the Habsburg Empire in the 1740s.

Haile Selassie, emperor of Ethiopia, was overthrown by the army in 1974.

BRITISH INDIA
Over 600 small states, ruled by leaders including rajahs and maharajahs, came under the British Empire in India. They had their own laws, armies and finances, but British troops were stationed in some states to ensure loyalty.

Some of the greatest empires in history were the Roman, Byzantine, Japanese, Ottoman, Russian and British empires. Each was ruled by an emperor or empress, but there have been other types of rule.

POWER GROWTH
Empires are usually built up when a country becomes richer or has larger armed forces than its neighbours, allowing it to spread its power and influence. The Greek king Alexander the Great trained his army with new weapons and tactics before conquering a vast empire from 334 to 323BC. The European Habsburg dynasty used royal marriages and treaties to expand its Holy Roman Empire for more than 300 years from the 15th century. In the 1800s, the British Empire was won by economic strength, backed up by military superiority when needed.

IMPERIAL RULE
Many empires are ruled by a single state or nation, often with great brutality. The Assyrians in the Ancient Middle East used their army to enforce the king's rule and to collect taxes. Those who disobeyed were cruelly punished. The Mongol Empire was run as a dictatorship in which the khan's wishes were enforced by the army. Other empires allowed some freedoms to their subjects. The states in the Athenian Empire of the 5th century BC met each year to discuss events. Many of the cities and states in the Holy Roman Empire were free to run their own affairs, make their own laws and even go to war.

KEY DATES

1500–1100BC Egyptian New Kingdom rules an empire in southwest Asia

850–609BC Assyrian Empire rules the Middle East.

559–326BC Persian Empire flourishes

264BC–AD410 Rome expands to rule vast areas before falling to barbarian invasion

228BC China united under the Qin Dynasty

AD800 Holy Roman Empire begins with the coronation of Charlemagne

1206 Genghis Khan founds the Mongol Empire

1492–1828 Spain conquers an empire in the Americas before colonies win independence

1880–1950s European powers build empires in Africa and Asia, then grant colonies independence

COLONIAL ADVENTURES

The Industrial Revolution made European states richer and better armed than other peoples. By 1850, several European nations owned colonies in Africa and Asia, which produced wealth and trade. In 1882, the British took over Egypt, prompting other European nations to conquer vast areas of Africa, Asia and the Pacific and turn them into colonies. Within 40 years, it became clear these new colonies produced little wealth, but were costly to maintain.

COLLAPSE OF EMPIRES

Empires may collapse as the result of foreign attack, member states breaking away or internal dispute. The Ancient Persian Empire was defeated in war by the Greeks under Alexander the Great. The Roman Empire was weakened by internal power struggles, and then fell to barbarian attacks in the 5th century. In 1917, the German and Habsburg Empires were divided up into smaller states by the victorious Allies at the end of World War I and the new states were racked by revolution, bringing an end to the Empires.

A POST-IMPERIAL WORLD

Since 1945, very few empires have continued to exist. The colonial empires of the British, French and other European

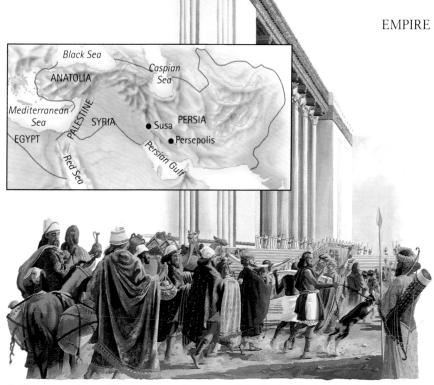

▲ The great palace of Persepolis was the centre of the Persian Empire, founded by Darius the Great in 559BC. Nations subject to the Persian 'King of Kings' brought tributes to Persepolis each spring as part of a great festival.

nations broke up when, weakened by World War II, they could not afford to keep the colonies in the face of nationalist independence movements. In 1990, the Soviet Union broke up as the states of the old Russian Empire declared themselves independent. There are few multi-national empires in the world today, because most nations are able to survive economically and do not need to be part of an empire to be protected from invaders.

▲ The Forbidden City, Beijing, was the Palace of the Chinese emperors from 1421 to 1911. It now houses museums and galleries.

◄ The Assyrian Empire, with its capital at Nineveh, was a military state based on cruel and constant warfare. It collapsed in 609BC when its enemies united to capture Nineveh.

SEE ALSO

Aztecs, Babylon, Incas, Mongols, Napoleonic Wars, Roman Empire

ENERGY

Energy is the ability to do work. An object or substance has energy if it can move or if it can generate such things as heat, sound, or electricity.

The Sun provides most of the heat and light energy that we use on Earth.

When anything moves, such as a car, it is using kinetic energy.

Dynamite's explosive power comes from stored chemical energy.

A radio produces sound energy by making the atoms in the air vibrate.

A hammer coming down to strike a nail uses the potential energy of gravity.

Nuclear energy takes its most dramatic form in a nuclear explosion.

Energy is everywhere – in sunlight as heat and light energy, in a CD player as sound energy, even in a lump of coal as stored chemical energy. Energy can be converted from one form into another, but it can never be destroyed.

MOVING OBJECTS

One of the most basic forms of energy is the energy of movement, or kinetic energy. Heavy, fast-moving objects have more kinetic energy than light, slow-moving ones. The kinetic energy of a car is less than that of a lorry travelling at the same speed. A parked car has no kinetic energy at all.

HEAT ENERGY

Kinetic energy is also closely related to heat energy. An object is hot because its atoms (the tiny particles that it is made of) are constantly in motion. So an object's heat energy can be thought of as the kinetic energy of its atoms. The faster its atoms move, the hotter the object becomes.

SAVING IT FOR LATER

Energy can be stored to be used later. This energy in storage is called potential energy.

▲ A runner waiting on the blocks to start a race is like a coiled spring ready to expand. When the starter's gun goes, the potential (stored) energy in the runner's muscles is converted into the kinetic (motion) energy of running.

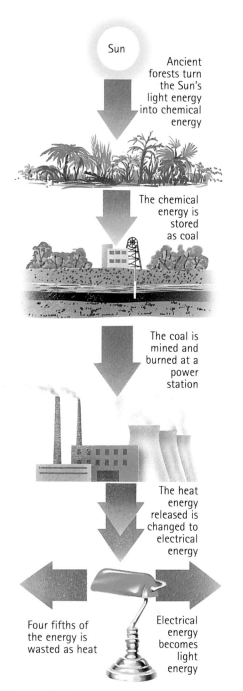

Sun

Ancient forests turn the Sun's light energy into chemical energy

The chemical energy is stored as coal

The coal is mined and burned at a power station

The heat energy released is changed to electrical energy

Four fifths of the energy is wasted as heat

Electrical energy becomes light energy

ENERGY CYCLE

The Sun is our main source of energy on Earth. Every time it is used, the energy changes form. Other natural sources include oil, gas and coal, but we use them wastefully.

A spring stores energy as it is squeezed. When it is released and expands back to its original shape, the potential energy becomes motion (kinetic energy).

CHANGING FORM

The law of conservation of energy says that energy can never be destroyed or lost, but will change its form. For example, if a boy gliding on a pair of roller-skates slowly comes to a halt, his kinetic energy will gradually decrease to zero. But the energy does not vanish, it is transformed into two other energy forms: heat and sound. The heat, created by the friction of the roller-skate wheels rubbing on the ground, warms up both the wheels and the ground. The sound energy can be heard as a swish or squeak of the wheels.

ENERGY AND POWER

Scientists measure energy using units called joules (J). Power – the rate at which energy is used – is measured in watts (W). The idea of power involves time. If two kettles heat a litre of water from 10°C to 100°C, they both give the water the same amount of heat energy. But if one kettle does the job in half the time, it has twice the amount of power as the other. Nuclear power works by releasing the energy locked up inside the nucleus of an atom and using it to do work.

MAKING IT WORK

Energy is never lost, but can be wasted if it is not put to work. Heat is the main cause of energy wastage. For example, an ordinary light bulb converts only one fifth of its electrical energy into light – the rest is wasted as heat. Inefficiency of car engines also means that the Earth's natural energy resources, such as oil, are constantly being wasted.

AN ENERGETIC GAME OF PINBALL

Energy is constantly changing its state. In a game of pinball, potential energy is converted into kinetic energy. The moving ball will tend to slow down through friction as it comes into contact with parts of the machine. Energy is used up in overcoming friction, but it is not lost – it is changed into heat. When the player adds energy to the ball, by pushing it with a flipper, the ball speeds up.

1 Pulling back the plunger coils a spring just behind the ball. In energy terms, the potential energy in the player's hand is transferred to the spring.

2 Letting go of the plunger shoots the ball into play. The spring's potential energy is changed into the kinetic energy of the moving ball.

3 As the ball moves inside the machine, it starts to slow down – its kinetic energy is being changed, mainly into heat. Flippers and obstacles have springs to speed the ball up.

SEE ALSO

Ecology, Electricity, Force and motion, Heat, Light, Magnetism, Nuclear power, Solar power, Sound

ENGINE

Engines are machines which convert energy into mechanical work to power vehicles, to drive other machines or to generate electricity.

The main types of engine are steam, petrol, diesel, jet and rocket. Each one is supplied with energy by burning, or combusting, fuels such as coal, petrol and diesel oil. Nearly all engines are internal combustion engines, which means the fuel is burnt inside the engine. The exception to this is the steam engine, which uses external combustion.

FRANK WHITTLE
(1907–87) An officer in the British Royal Air Force, he built the first successful jet engine, known as a gas turbine.

EARLY STEAM ENGINES
In the 18th century, much of the power for the Industrial Revolution was provided by the steam engine. In 1712, Englishman Thomas Newcomen developed the first practical steam engine for pumping water from mines. In 1765, a Scottish engineer, James Watt, began to improve the Newcomen steam engine and developed a much more efficient machine. Soon steam engines were powering factory machinery, as well as railway vehicles such as the *Rocket* locomotive, built by English engineer George Stephenson in 1829.

▲ A microlite is a hang-glider with an engine. It uses a two-stroke engine, which is lighter, cheaper and more powerful for its size than a four-stroke engine.

THE POWER OF STEAM
In a steam engine, a fire is used to boil water to produce high-pressure steam. As the steam expands, it pushes a piston to and fro in a cylinder, or turns the blades of a fan-like wheel called a turbine. These then drive the machine. Most steam engines have been replaced by internal combustion engines. However, many power station generators today are still worked by steam turbines.

PETROL ENGINES
Nowadays, cars, trucks, buses and many trains and aircraft use internal combustion

WERNHER VON BRAUN
(1912–77) He was head of the team of German scientists that created the V2 – the first rocket-powered guided missile, and the inspiration for later moon rockets.

STEAM LOCOMOTIVE

Steam locomotives powered the railways of the world for over 130 years. Hot gases from the burning coal surround the water tubes, turning the water to steam. The steam passes to the cylinder, driving the piston backwards and forwards. The piston in turn pushes the connecting rod backwards and forwards, which rotates a crank and drives the wheels. Water and coal are carried in the tender.

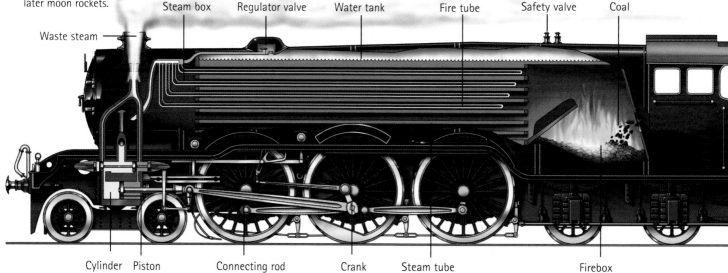

Waste steam — Steam box — Regulator valve — Water tank — Fire tube — Safety valve — Coal

Cylinder — Piston — Connecting rod — Crank — Steam tube — Firebox

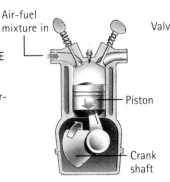
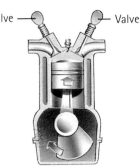

A FOUR-STROKE ENGINE
Cars have internal combustion engines with pistons that work in a four-stroke cycle (the piston makes two movements up and two down). Air and fuel are let into the piston cylinder by valves at the top. The explosion of ignited fuel moves the piston, which turns a crankshaft. This spins the drive shaft.

Labels: Air-fuel mixture in, Piston, Crank shaft, Valve, Valve, Spark plug, Exhaust gas out

1 **Induction.** As the piston goes down, it draws a mixture of air and petrol into the cylinder.

2 **Compression.** The piston rises, squashing the fuel and air mixture ready for ignition.

3 **Power.** A spark lights the fuel, forcing the piston down and turning the crankshaft.

4 **Exhaust.** On the final stroke of the engine, the piston rises to expel exhaust (waste) gases.

engines fuelled by diesel oil or petrol. In a petrol engine, the fuel mixes with air inside a cylinder, and a spark sets the mixture alight, pushing the piston up and down in a four-stroke cycle (see above).

DIESEL ENGINES
Like petrol engines, diesel engines have cylinders, pistons, valves and a fuel supply, but there are no spark plugs or ignition system. The fuel explodes because of the immense heat created when the piston compresses the fuel and air inside a cylinder. The explosion of fuel pushes the piston up and down, powering the vehicle.

THE GAS TURBINE
A jet, or gas-turbine, engine does not have pistons. Instead, air is sucked in at the front of the engine and compressed, or squashed, by the rotating blades of the compressor. The air is blown into the combustion chamber and ignited with aviation fuel. The hot gases are expelled from the back of the engine, pushing the plane forward.

TO THE STARS
Like jet engines, rocket engines also use their exhaust gases to push the vehicle forward. Unlike jets, however, rockets cannot burn fuel by taking in oxygen from the air, as there is no air in space. Instead, they carry their oxygen supply with them, usually as liquid oxygen. The fuel either ignites spontaneously when mixed with the oxygen, or is lit by a spark.

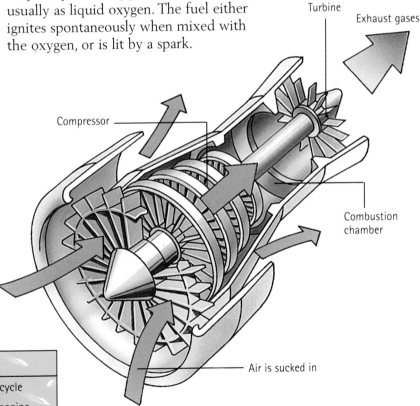

Labels: Turbine, Exhaust gases, Compressor, Combustion chamber, Air is sucked in

A JET ENGINE
In a jet aeroplane engine, air is sucked in at the front of the engine by giant rotating blades. The air is then compressed and passed into a combustion (burning) chamber, where it is ignited. The plane is thrust forward by the exhaust gases. These gases also turn a turbine, which drives the compressor.

KEY DATES
1862 Alphonse Beau de Rochas invents the four-stroke cycle
1876 Nikolaus Otto develops the prototype automobile engine
1878 Sir Dougald Clerk invents the two-stroke cycle
1892 Rudolph Diesel patents the diesel engine
1930s C. P. Steinmetz's *Future of Electricity* predicts air pollution from use of coal as fuel
1939 The first jet-engined aircraft, the Heinkel, flies in Germany
1944 The first V2 missile is fired on enemy targets

SEE ALSO
Aircraft, Car, Electricity, Energy, Rocket, Train, Transport

EUROPE

Europe is the second smallest of the world's seven continents. It has 45 countries, including parts of Russia, Turkey and Kazakhstan.

KEY FACTS

- **Area:** 22,986,000 sq km
- **Population:** 704,000,000
- **Number of countries:** 45
- **Largest country:** Russia, 25 per cent (4,309,400 sq km) of which is in Europe
- **Smallest country:** Vatican City (0.44 sq km)
- **Highest point:** Mount Elbrus (5,642m)
- **Largest lake:** Lake Ladoga (17,700 sq km)
- **Longest river:** Volga (3,688km)

Only the continent of Australia is smaller than Europe, but Europe's moderate climate, rich resources and fertile land support a large population. Between them, the people speak about 50 languages and many more dialects. With its 45 countries, Europe is a continent of diverse cultures.

NEVER FAR FROM WATER
The northwest and west of Europe are bordered by the Arctic and Atlantic Oceans, while the Mediterranean Sea surrounds the south. The coastline is broken up by thousands of fjords and other inlets and only nine European countries have no access to the sea.

NORTH EUROPEAN PLAIN
Many of Europe's most populated areas lie on the North European Plain, which stretches from the southern part of the United Kingdom through northern France, Germany and Poland to the Ural Mountains in Russia. To the north are

▲ Iceland in the North Atlantic Ocean is known as the Land of Ice and Fire because of its volcanoes and hot springs set against a landscape of ice fields and glaciers.

forests of coniferous trees such as fir, larch and pine. Deciduous forests of ash, elm and oak grow in central and southern Europe. In the southeast are large areas of dry grassland called steppes.

SCANDINAVIA
In the far north of Europe lies the cold and mountainous region of Scandinavia, which includes the countries of Norway, Sweden, Denmark and Finland. The climate around the Arctic Ocean is cold and snowy, with temperatures in January averaging below –16°C. Few trees grow in the extreme north, but the forests farther south contain large animals such as brown bears, reindeer and wolves.

▼ Wine is produced throughout Europe, particularly in France (shown here), Germany, Spain, Italy and Bulgaria.

miles
0   500
0   500
km

N

ARCTIC OCEAN

ICELAND

NORWEGIAN SEA

NORWAY

SWEDEN

FINLAND

Lake Ladoga

RUSSIA (European part)

Ural Mountains

NORTH SEA

DENMARK

BALTIC SEA

ESTONIA

LATVIA

LITHUANIA

RUSSIA

UNITED KINGDOM

IRELAND

EUROPEAN PLAIN

BELARUS

KAZAKHSTAN (European part)

1

NORTH

GERMANY

POLAND

UKRAINE

Volga

ATLANTIC OCEAN

2

CZECH REPUBLIC

SLOVAKIA

Carpathian Mts.

5

4

AUSTRIA

HUNGARY

16

Caspian Sea

FRANCE

Alps

10

11

ROMANIA

Mt. Elbrus

Pyrenees

7

6

9

12

13

BLACK SEA

PORTUGAL

8

BULGARIA

Bosporus

SPAIN

ITALY

14

TURKEY (European part)

MEDITERRANEAN SEA

15

GREECE

MALTA

KEY TO MAP
1 THE NETHERLANDS
2 BELGIUM
3 LUXEMBOURG
4 SWITZERLAND
5 LIECHTENSTEIN
6 MONACO
7 ANDORRA
8 VATICAN CITY
9 SAN MARINO
10 SLOVENIA
11 CROATIA
12 BOSNIA-HERZEGOVINA
13 YUGOSLAVIA
14 MACEDONIA
15 ALBANIA
16 MOLDOVA

THE MEDITERRANEAN

The southern part of Europe is divided from the north by three mountain ranges: the Pyrenees, the Alps and the Carpathian Mountains. The Mediterranean countries of southern Europe, including Italy, Spain and Greece, have mild, rainy winters and hot, dry summers.

A FERTILE CONTINENT

Europe is a fertile continent with farms covering more than half the land. Crops include barley, oats, potatoes and wheat, and citrus fruits and olives in the south. Vast areas of steppes in southern Russia and Ukraine and are farmed for grain.

OIL, GAS AND COAL

Oil and natural gas are produced in the North Sea, and coal is found in large quantities in Europe. These fuels help power the continent's many factories – Europe produces more manufactured goods than any other continent, including cars, electronic goods, ships and steel.

A MIXED POPULATION

Most Europeans are the descendants of people who lived on the continent in prehistoric times, but there is a long history of immigration from Africa, Asia and the Caribbean region. About 70 per cent of the population lives in cities and towns, working in factories or service industries, such as finance and tourism. ▶

▲ The number of red squirrels has decreased in Europe in the 20th century, following the introduction of the grey squirrel from North America and loss of large areas of woodland.

BRANCHES OF CHRISTIANITY

Christianity is Europe's leading religion. Many follow the Roman Catholic Church, which has its headquarters in Vatican City. The Vatican covers just 0.44 sq km in Rome, Italy, and is the world's smallest independent country. Protestantism is a branch of Christianity popular in northern Europe, while the Orthodox Church flourishes in the east and southeast.

HISTORICAL CITIES

Many of Europe's large cities are steeped in history, but are also characterized by modern architecture and a modern way of life. Paris in France contains magnificent buildings dating from the Middle Ages, and is at the same time a leading fashion centre. Moscow in Russia and London in the UK are important international cities, as well as historic sites. Athens and Rome, the capitals of Greece and Italy, have impressive ruins surviving from the days of Ancient Greece and the Roman Empire.

DEMOCRACY AND LAW

Throughout history, Europe has had an important influence on world politics. The system of democracy – where the government is chosen by the people – was first tried in Ancient Greece about 2,500 years ago. Similarly, many of the

▲ Istanbul in Turkey lies on the shores of the Bosporus, which divides Europe from Asia. Its buildings reflect a mixture of Eastern and Western styles.

▲ The ruins of Delphi, a sacred site from as early as 1100BC, stand on Mount Parnassus in the southern part of mainland Greece.

laws developed during the Roman civilization (from 590BC to AD476) still influence legal systems today.

THE RENAISSANCE

From the 1300s, Europe became an increasingly important centre of art and learning, with people interested in new ideas about art, science and literature. This period is known as the Renaissance. At the same time, a desire for trade led European seafarers to set out to explore unknown lands and later to start colonies abroad. In the late 18th century, the continent was the birthplace of the Industrial Revolution, which brought great power and prosperity to the West.

END OF EMPIRES

The map of Europe has often changed throughout history, largely because of wars between rival countries. In the 20th century, two great world wars were fought between European powers. In the years following World War II (1939–45), the empires created in African and Asia by European countries such as Belgium,

◄ Many European countries, such as Germany, the Netherlands, Romania and Italy, have strong national football teams and attract keen supporters such as these from Switzerland.

Britain, France, the Netherlands and Portugal came to an end. Former colonies became independent countries, but many people living there continued to follow European customs and speak European languages. A large number of them have since made their homes in Europe.

EAST AND WEST

By the 1950s, Europe was divided between the non-communist countries of the west and the Soviet-backed communist countries of the east. Until the 1980s, the two sides remained armed and

▲ After World War II, about a seventh of Berlin was in ruins. The city was divided between East and West until 1990, when Germany was reunited.

hostile throughout the period known as the Cold War. But from the late 1980s, the Eastern European countries threw off their communist governments following the break-up of the Soviet Union in 1991. Yugoslavia also split up into five separate countries at this time, and a new map of Europe was shaped, with new countries and partnerships.

◄ German car-making factories are among the most highly automated in the world, and the cars they produce are exported worldwide.

THE EUROPEAN UNION

In the 1950s, a group of countries in western Europe set up the European Community, or Common Market, to encourage greater economic unity in Europe. Over the years, the Community grew into the European Union, which aims for both economic and political unity. As of 2004, there are 25 member states.

SEE ALSO

Eastern Europe, France, Germany, Greece and the Balkans, Italy, Netherlands, Belgium and Luxembourg, Scandinavia, Spain and Portugal, Switzerland and Austria, UK

EVOLUTION

Evolution is the way in which an organism changes over many generations, resulting in a species that is very different from its early ancestors.

JEAN BAPTISTE LAMARCK (1744–1829) was a French biologist who believed, mistakenly, that animals evolved during their own lifetimes. For example, each giraffe, by stretching, elongated its neck.

CHARLES DARWIN (1809–1882) shook the world, and especially the Church, with his theory of natural selection, which he published in *On the Origin of Species* in 1859.

Most scientists believe that the first simple organisms appeared on Earth over 3,000 million years ago and that all today's plants and animals have arisen from these by a process of gradual change. This process, which is constantly happening from one generation to the next, is known as evolution.

DARWIN'S THEORY
The idea of evolution has been around since the time of the Ancient Greeks. However, the first convincing theory of how evolution works was only provided in the middle of the 19th century by the English naturalist Charles Darwin. He recognized that plants and animals produce lots of offspring but that only a small number of these offspring survive. Darwin concluded that only the individual with the most useful characteristics is able to survive in a process that he called the struggle for existence.

SURVIVAL OF THE FITTEST
Darwin noticed that individuals that are not well suited to their surroundings die out. This leaves only the fittest individuals

to breed and pass the useful characteristics that have allowed them to survive on to their offspring. In popular terms, this process is known as 'the survival of the fittest'. It explains the enormous variety of plant and animal life that is found throughout the world – because the conditions vary from place to place, animals and plants adapt to fit their environment.

LITTLE BY LITTLE
With each new generation of plant and animal life, the struggle for existence continues. The result is that, over a long period of time, plants and animals gradually change and become better

THE EVOLUTION OF MAN
The earliest human beings probably evolved from ape-like creatures such as *Ramapithecus* (15 mya). *Australopithecus* (3.75 mya) walked upright on his back legs. *Homo habilis* (2 mya) made basic tools from stone and bone, while *Homo erectus* (1.75 mya) was probably the first human being to use fire. The Neanderthal people (*Homo sapiens*, 40,000 ya) lived alongside *Homo sapiens sapiens* who developed into modern man.

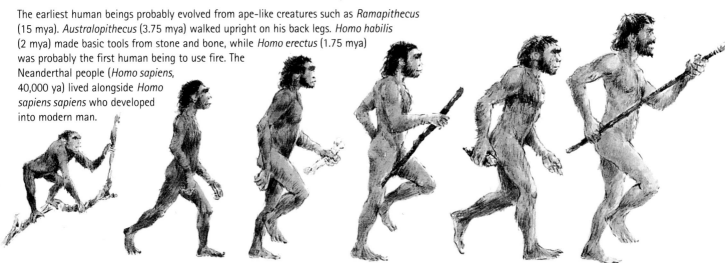

RAMAPITHECUS   AUSTRALOPITHECUS   HOMO HABILIS   HOMO ERECTUS   NEANDERTHAL MAN   HOMO SAPIENS SAPIENS

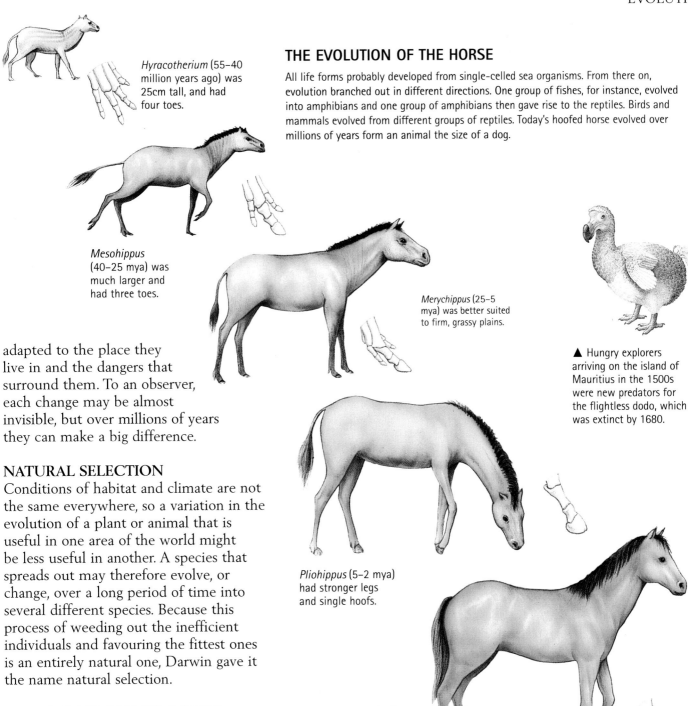

Hyracotherium (55–40 million years ago) was 25cm tall, and had four toes.

Mesohippus (40–25 mya) was much larger and had three toes.

Merychippus (25–5 mya) was better suited to firm, grassy plains.

Pliohippus (5–2 mya) had stronger legs and single hoofs.

Equus caballus (1.5 mya) was similar to today's horses.

▲ Hungry explorers arriving on the island of Mauritius in the 1500s were new predators for the flightless dodo, which was extinct by 1680.

THE EVOLUTION OF THE HORSE

All life forms probably developed from single-celled sea organisms. From there on, evolution branched out in different directions. One group of fishes, for instance, evolved into amphibians and one group of amphibians then gave rise to the reptiles. Birds and mammals evolved from different groups of reptiles. Today's hoofed horse evolved over millions of years form an animal the size of a dog.

adapted to the place they live in and the dangers that surround them. To an observer, each change may be almost invisible, but over millions of years they can make a big difference.

NATURAL SELECTION

Conditions of habitat and climate are not the same everywhere, so a variation in the evolution of a plant or animal that is useful in one area of the world might be less useful in another. A species that spreads out may therefore evolve, or change, over a long period of time into several different species. Because this process of weeding out the inefficient individuals and favouring the fittest ones is an entirely natural one, Darwin gave it the name natural selection.

EVIDENCE FROM THE ROCKS

Some of the strongest support for the idea of evolution comes from the fossilized remains of plants and animals that are found in rocks formed from layers of sand and mud on ancient sea beds. In each layer of rock, the organisms look slightly different from the ones below. This provides the evidence for a process of change over hundreds, thousands or even millions of years.

A COMMON ANCESTOR

The bone structure of living animals also gives clues to evolution. A human arm, a

bird's wings and a whale's flipper all look very different and have different uses in everyday life. However, their bones are actually very similar. This suggests that these animals have all evolved from a common ancestor, which spread out over a wide geographical area. The arms were then adapted for different jobs according to the demands of the different environments.

SEE ALSO

Dinosaur, Fossil, Genetics, Horse, Prehistoric animal, Prehistoric people

EXPLORER

**People explore to discover the unknown. Through
exploration we have learnt much about the Earth. We
are still exploring the oceans and the vastness of space.**

Christopher Columbus
opened up America to
European trade in 1492.

Captain Robert Scott died
on the way back from the
South Pole in 1912.

Jacques Cousteau helped
invent the aqualung so he
could explore underwater.

The Phoenicians were among the first
explorers, sailing the Mediterranean
around 3,000 years ago. Pytheas, a Greek
sailor, ventured into the Atlantic Ocean in
300BC and, in AD1000, Norway's Leif
Ericsson reached North America.

THE SILK ROAD

Chinese and Arab travellers made long
journeys overland. In 138BC, Zhang Qian
became the first Chinese man to explore
Central Asia. Later, European merchants
took the Silk Road to China, visited by the
Italian Marco Polo in 1275 and described
in his book, *Description of the World*.

AGE OF DISCOVERY

In the 15th century, stronger ships and the
invention of navigational aids such as the
backstaff (used to plot the ship's position
by the Sun and stars) prompted European
explorers to head to sea. They went in
search of lands to conquer and for trade,
riches and slaves. Seeking a sea route to
India, Portuguese sailors headed south
along the African coast. In 1488,
Bartholomeu Días reached the southern tip
of Africa, and in 1498, Vasco da Gama
crossed the Indian Ocean. Columbus
arrived in America from Spain in 1492.

MAP-MAKERS

In 1522, Ferdinand Magellan's ship from
Spain completed the first voyage around
the world. He died on the way, but the
trip proved that the Earth was round. In
the 1770s, James Cook, of the British
navy, sailed the Pacific, mapping the coast
of New Zealand and landing in Australia.

LAST FRONTIERS

Later explorers moved inland. The Scot
David Livingstone travelled into Africa.
Others ventured into uninhabited areas.
The American Robert Peary conquered the
North Pole in 1909, and Norway's Roald
Amundsen reached the South Pole
in 1911. In 1960, the bathyscaphe *Trieste*
dived 10,910m under the sea, and in
1969, man walked on the Moon.

INTO THE UNKNOWN

Early sea voyages advanced navigational knowledge and helped map-makers to produce
more accurate maps. In the 1400s, Henry the Navigator, a Portuguese prince skilled in
mathematics and astronomy, helped organize 50 expeditions to West Africa. These trips
pushed back the frontiers of navigation and paved the way for future trade and exploration.

SEE ALSO

Antarctica, Asia, Australia,
Map, Ocean and sea,
Space exploration,
Submarine, Vikings